T0360507

Business Models

The growing body of research on business models draws upon a range of sub-disciplines, including strategic management, entrepreneurship, organization studies and management accounting.

Business Models: A Research Overview provides a research map for business scholars, incorporating theoretical and applied perspectives. It develops the field of business model research by offering a critique of the field as it has developed to date and provides a guide for future research and theorization. The research performed as a basis for this book improves and extends prior subjective and less-documented work by using a scientific approach to identifying impactful research. The book argues that business model research is a mature field and that future research should focus on performative and ecosystem-based contributions, with the timely identification of four distinct stages of business model research. The study here provokes a new set of research questions, which are addressed in the concluding passages of Chapters 5–8, as a point of departure for those researching business models.

This book is essential primary reading for scholars and practitioners of business models who are looking to seek out new knowledge and build new perspectives.

Christian Nielsen is Professor at the Department of Business and Management, Aalborg University, Denmark. Christian currently serves as Head of Department as well as being Co-Editor-in-Chief of the *Journal of Business Models*. He is a global thought leader in the design of scalable business models.

Morten Lund is Associate Professor and Director of the Business Design Center at Aalborg University, Denmark. Morten is an experienced entrepreneur and executive manager who has founded, consulted on and invested in multiple ventures with disruptive business models. He holds a Ph.D. in Business Models.

Marco Montemari is Assistant Professor at the Università Politecnica delle Marche, Italy. His research interests concern management accounting, intellectual capital and business models. Marco's research has been published in the *Journal of Intellectual Capital* and the *European Journal of Innovation Management*, among others.

Francesco Paolone holds a degree in Business Administration from Bocconi University, Italy. He is currently a postdoctoral researcher at Parthenope University of Naples. His research profiles are focused on financial reporting, corporate governance and business models. He is the author of several international scientific contributions.

Maurizio Massaro is Associate Professor at Ca' Foscari University of Venice and Udine University, Italy. One of Maurizio's articles has recently been awarded the Emerald Literati Award for Excellence. He is a member of the Global Most Innovative Knowledge Enterprise (MIKE) Award as the Italian representative.

John Dumay is Professor of Accounting and Finance, Macquarie University, Sydney, Australia, and a highly cited author of over 100 peer-reviewed articles, book chapters and conference papers. His Ph.D. *Intellectual Capital in Action: Australian Studies* won the Emerald/EFMD Outstanding Doctoral Research Award in 2008 for Knowledge Management.

State of the Art in Business Research
Edited by Professor Geoffrey Wood

Recent advances in theory, methods and applied knowledge (alongside structural changes in the global economic ecosystem) have presented researchers with challenges in seeking to stay abreast of their fields and navigate new scholarly terrains.

State of the Art in Business Research presents shortform books which provide an expert map to guide readers through new and rapidly evolving areas of research. Each title will provide an overview of the area, a guide to the key literature and theories and time-saving summaries of how theory interacts with practice.

As a collection, these books provide a library of theoretical and conceptual insights, and exposure to novel research tools and applied knowledge, that aid and facilitate in defining the state of the art, as a foundation stone for a new generation of research.

Print ISSN: 2575-4815; Online ISSN: 2575-4807

Business and the Natural Environment
A Research Overview
Andrew Hoffman and Susse Georg

Nonprofit Marketing and Fundraising
A Research Overview
Roger Bennett

Mergers and Acquisitions
A Research Overview
David R. King, Florian Bauer and Svante Schriber

Business Models
A Research Overview
Christian Nielsen, Morten Lund, Marco Montemari, Francesco Paolone, Maurizio Massaro and John Dumay

Business Models
A Research Overview

Christian Nielsen, Morten Lund, Marco Montemari, Francesco Paolone, Maurizio Massaro and John Dumay

Routledge
Taylor & Francis Group

LONDON AND NEW YORK

First published 2019
by Routledge
2 Park Square, Milton Park, Abingdon, Oxon OX14 4RN

and by Routledge
52 Vanderbilt Avenue, New York, NY 10017

Routledge is an imprint of the Taylor & Francis Group, an informa business

British Library Cataloguing-in-Publication Data
A catalogue record for this book is available from the British Library

Library of Congress Cataloging-in-Publication Data
A catalog record has been requested for this book

ISBN: 978-0-8153-7851-8 (hbk)
ISBN: 978-1-351-23227-2 (ebk)

Typeset in Times New Roman
by codeMantra

Contents

Figures

Tables

Foreword

The field of business models has undergone an immense development in the last decade, and chances are that this is going to continue at ever more accelerating speeds in the years to come.

At the beginning of the 2000s, together with Alexander Osterwalder, we defined an ontology of business models; then we created the *Business Model Canvas*, which became the foundation for our co-authored bestseller *Business Model Generation*. This book and the canvas marked a turning point for the field of business models because it convened academic insights with practitioner needs. I believe this is the core strength of the field of business models, and this is also evident in this present contribution, which in many instances highlights this crucial connection. After all, if academics cannot provide insights that company owners and managers can apply towards improving their organizations, then what are they good for?

Who better than Christian Nielsen and his colleagues to write this state of the art of business model research? Dear readers and researchers, let yourselves be charmed by this novel and timely contribution to business model research.

Yves Pigneur
Professor at the University of Lausanne and
Co-Author with Alex Osterwalder of
Business Model Generation

Acknowledgements

The authors wish to thank participants at the Business Model Leadership seminar and the 1st Business Model Conference in Venice, 17–19 May 2017, as well as the participants at the 2nd Business Model Conference in Florence, 5–6 June 2018, for their comments and suggestions. Furthermore, we would also like to thank participants at the Future Research Directions in Business Models seminar with Charles Baden-Fuller, hosted by Business Design Center on 5 October 2017 in Aalborg, for fruitful discussions. Further thanks go to Jesper Sort, Peter Thomsen, Christian Byrge, Kristian Brøndum, Erik Bjurström, Torben Toft Kristensen, Martin Krogstrup Nielsen and Robin Roslender for comments on previous versions of the manuscript. Finally, we wish to thank Fiona Crawford for proofreading assistance and Thor F. Jensen for graphical reproductions.

1 The rising relevance of understanding business models

Growing attention around the business model concept is based on the combination of two major factors that have arisen over the last 25 years and radically changed the competitive landscape. First, the advent of the digital era and new information and communication technologies have disrupted traditional ways of doing business and unlocked new ways of creating value. For example, in industries like transportation (Uber), accommodation (Airbnb), music (Spotify), retail (Amazon) and telecommunications (Skype), where new agile technology-based businesses using mainly bits and bytes have replaced traditional bricks and mortar businesses.

Second, hyper-dynamic and globalized markets have forced companies to rethink and innovate how they do business. A notable example is that of Apple, which has integrated its initial offerings of personal computers with music delivery devices and services, including mobile phones.

Against this constantly changing landscape, from the late 20th century, a new concept, the business model, has gradually arisen as one of the fundamental drivers to create, maintain and expand competitive advantage. As such, it must be carefully designed and constantly updated. Awareness that companies do not create value in the same way, and that the features of the business model significantly affect performance, has gradually attracted significant attention to this concept, as evidenced by the proliferation of frameworks and tools for business model design (Chatterjee, 2013; Casadesus-Masanell and Ricart, 2011) and innovation (Gassmann *et al.*, 2014; Taran *et al.*, 2016), the use of business models in companies and the spate of recent reviews of the business model (Foss and Saebi, 2017; Wirtz *et al.*, 2016b).

The two words making up the term 'business model' have specific meanings: a 'business' is the activity of providing goods and services, involving financial, commercial and industrial aspects. A 'model' is a simplified description and representation of a complex entity or process. By joining the two words, Osterwalder *et al.* (2005, p. 3) provides a general definition:

> A business model is a conceptual tool containing a set of objects, concepts and their relationships with the objective to express the business logic of a specific firm. Therefore, we must consider which concepts and relationships allow a simplified description and representation of what value is provided to customers, how this is done and with which financial consequences.

Several prior definitions (Galper, 2001; Gebauer and Ginsburg, 2003) indicate a constant use of the 'business model' term in regard to the way in which companies do business, highlighting the way the model is used to reduce complexity to an understandable level (Osterwalder, 2004; Taran *et al.*, 2016). In sum, the essence of the business model is that it identifies the elements and relationships that describe how companies do business.

It is worth noting that there is still no generally accepted definition of what a business model is, but there is consensus about the description of a business model as the framework through which companies implement their strategy (McGrath, 2010; Nielsen and Montemari, 2012; Nielsen *et al.*, 2009), thus clarifying how value is created and captured (Osterwalder and Pigneur, 2010; Teece, 2010). In particular, the business model concept views a company as a set of interrelated decisions that concern its main strategic elements, such as the value proposition, along with the activities, resources and partners required to develop the value proposition itself, as well as target customers and the channels and relationships needed to reach the customers themselves (Morris *et al.*, 2005). Thus, the business model concept is valuable for managers and entrepreneurs as it enables the comprehension of the value creation process and the identification of the value drivers that arise as strategy is being executed (Montemari and Chiucchi, 2017).

This introduction outlines the reasons for the development of the business model and why it is a concept worthy of analysis. The following sections discuss the initial stages of the business model research area and the drivers that have made the business model concept popular over time.

Brief history and popularity drivers across time

This chapter outlines the state of the art in the field of business models. First it looks at some important initial phases in the research area by shedding light on the origins of the term 'business model', on the contexts where it has been used and on the meanings that it was initially given.

The term 'business model' was first mentioned in 1957 by Bellman *et al.* in their article analyzing the construction of business games for training purposes. The term was cited just once: "And many more problems arise to plague us in the construction of these business models than ever confronted an engineer" (Bellman *et al.*, 1957, p. 474). This mention seems to relate the business model concept to a simplified representation of the real world though a model.

Three years later, Jones (1960) published the first academic article using 'business model' in its title; however, the term was not mentioned further within the paper, which was aimed at addressing some questions about how college students should be trained and how technologies should support them.

During the 1960s there were a number of discussions concerning the interrelationships among strategy, organizational structure and technologies from a business model perspective. The origins of the business model concept can be traced back to Chandler's seminal book *Strategy and Structure* from 1962, where strategy is defined as "the determination of the basic long-term goals and objectives of an enterprise, and the adoption of courses of action and the allocation of resources necessary for carrying out these goals" (Chandler, 1962, p. 13). Here Chandler's focus is on execution, which implicitly highlights the relevance of the business model concept; new strategic decisions, like becoming diversified or expanding the volume of activities, entail not only new strategic goals, but also new courses of actions and a revised allocation of resources. Thompson's *Organizations in Action* from 1967 is a seminal contribution with respect to technology's impact from a business model perspective. In particular, Thompson proposes a typology of different kinds of organizational technologies, distinguishing between long-linked, intensive and mediating technologies. These different technology types play different roles in connection with value creation as well as structuring of companies and their value chains.

Further developments in the concept are seen in Andrews' distinction between corporate and business strategy (Andrews, 1971): the former defines the businesses in which a company competes, its goals and the plans to achieve these goals, as well as the nature of its human and economic organization that it aims to convert from distinctive competences into competitive advantage; the latter determines how a company competes in a given business and its position compared to competitors, namely the choice of products or services and the market for individual businesses.

By referring to Chandler's work, Child's paper from 1972 on "Organizational structure, environment and performance: The role of strategic choice" is one of the earliest to gather and present these thoughts diagrammatically. Although Child does use the term business model within his schema of "The role of strategic choice in a theory of organization" (Child, 1972, p. 18), the thoughts presented incorporate many of the central elements presented within the recent literature on this emerging concept. For instance, Child's term "prior ideology" covers the aspects of an organization's vision and value proposition, objectives and strategy, while "operating effectiveness" is viewed as an outcome of the organizational strategy and the elements scale of operations, technology, structure and human resources.

A commonly stated adage is that having an adaptive organization is essential to survive in today's competitive business environment. Starbuck and Dutton commented as early as 1973, that the "central issue in designing adaptive organizations is to choose strategies and structures that will allow organizations to exploit their environments" (Starbuck and Dutton, 1973, p. 166). Chandler's influence is clear.

While the notion of strategy has subsequently developed in a myriad of directions, one branch of its development that prefigures the argument here is research into how managers can leverage the resources of an organization beyond that organization's current business. For example, Prahalad and Bettis (1986), in their account of the link between diversity and performance, describe how mental maps developed in the core business are applicable in, for example, other divisions of an enterprise as representations of top management's ideals. This example shows the richness and diversity of perspectives relating to business models.

This brief review shows that for several decades the term 'business model' had no real prominence in the literature or in practice. This changed in the second half of the 1990s, when a significant increase in the usage of the term emerged with the 'dot-com' period (Mahadevan, 2000; Rappa, 2004; Slywotsky, 1996; Timmers, 1998). Figure 1 clearly illustrates this phenomenon, by depicting the increasing use of the term in the Google Scholar database between 1980 and 2017.

Already at the turn of the millennium, there was a lot of awareness around a globalizing, fast-communicating world. "The nature of business had changed", was a common exclamation, and arguments relating to globalization of markets, greater mobility of the workforce, the application of information technology (IT) and technologies in general were readily thrown into debate among academics and practitioners, and in the media (Hand, 2001). The aforementioned factors,

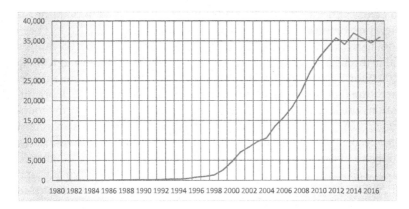

Figure 1 Use of the term 'business model' in the Google Scholar database (1980–2017).

among others, seemed to generate significant changes in the nature of value creation. In addition, intangible assets and knowledge resources had become ever more important for companies to manage and utilize (Arthur, 1994; Drucker, 1993). In the 'new economy', intangibles rather than physical and financial capital had become the pivotal factor underlying value creation (Bontis, 2001; Eustace, 2000).

From an economics perspective, wealth creation was often referred to as being more dynamic in the new economy. In 2001, Schmid (2001, p. 44) argued that the design of value creation systems was challenged as new forces, for example, IT, were changing the structures of the economy. Evans and Wurster (1997, p. 19) reasoned that "the changing economics of information threaten to undermine established value chains in many sectors of the economy, requiring virtually every company to rethink its strategy – not incrementally, but fundamentally".

Palenzuela (2001) confirmed the observed industrial restructuring mentioned previously, highlighting that sources of economic renewal, that is, wealth creation, increasingly derive from knowledge-based industries rather than traditional industries. In continuation of this line of reasoning, such changes in the nature of value creation inevitably place pressure on the way companies understand themselves, their role in industrial value chains and the way they communicate about their activities (see also Feng *et al.*, 2001).

The term 'business model' has been predominantly connected with e-business (e.g. Alt and Zimmermann, 2001; Kodama, 1999; Mahadevan, 2000; Timmers, 1998), as the application of the Internet has caused a revolution in possible ways of doing business and unlocked the potential to create an array of new business models. A major focal point of the literature on business models from an e-business perspective has been how to migrate successfully to e-business models and how to capture value through e-business models (see, for example, Hedman and Kalling (2003) for a thorough review). Therefore, much of the business model literature focusing on the e-business context concerns how such organizations can create value in comparison to their bricks and mortar counterparts (Alt and Zimmermann, 2001; Rappa, 2001). There is an almost unprecedented number of ways of creating business opportunities by applying IT to existing business concepts. Rappa (2001) has conducted an extensive review of business models on the Web, identifying a total of 29 different e-business models distributed across nine industry-based categories.

Amit and Zott (2001) identify four interdependent dimensions of value creation potential in e-businesses. For an e-business model to be profitable, it must create efficiencies in comparison to existing ways of doing business, facilitate complementarities and/or novelty or enable the lock-in of customers. For example, the creation of efficiencies is precisely the underlying notion of Internet-based business models in the banking industry (DeYoung, 2005), while Gallaugher (2002) illustrates how e-commerce as a new distribution channel has created efficiencies, thus enabling new business models.

As indicated by Alt and Zimmermann (2001, p. 1), "much talk revolves around how traditional business models are being changed and the future of e-based business models". However, this is merely half the story. Business models are perhaps the most discussed and least understood of the newer business concepts, although many enterprises do not have clearly articulated or presented business models (Shipley, 1995). Furthermore, Alt and Zimmermann (2001) conclude that there is an incomplete and confusing picture of the dimensions, perspectives and core issues of the business model concept (Arendt, 2013). There is no clear definition of what a business model is and which characteristics and components such a model should incorporate. As Porter (2001, p. 73) states, "The definition of a business model is murky at best". Similarly, Hedman and Kalling (2001) acknowledge that a theoretically sound definition of the business model does not exist at present.

Starting from these considerations, with the turn of the millennium, some attempts to portray the business model as an independent concept began to appear, the aim being to distinguish it from established concepts, such as strategy or business planning.

In 2000, Gary Hamel, in his book *Leading the Revolution* (p. 15), argued for the need to look beyond competition between firms in similar segments to viewing competitive strategy on the level of whole business concepts, also labelled value networks or value chains, that is, as competing business models. Working with the concept of the business model can help management obtain an understanding of the nuances of the business and to envisage the connection to the company's competitive strategy (Sandberg, 2002). Magretta (2002, p. 6) also posits this, although stressing that a company's business model and competitive strategy is not the same. According to Magretta, the role of the business model is to describe how the pieces of the business fit together, while competitive strategy concerns how the business will do better than its competitors.

In parallel, the concept was becoming more popular and established itself outside the sphere of Internet commerce. Hence, every firm was recognized as having a business model (Katkalo, 2008; Stewart and Zhao, 2000) and this led to an increase in the number of publications describing business models and employing a given author's own definition of the business model, its key components and schemes for analysis (Amit and Zott, 2001; Chesbrough and Rosenbloom, 2002; Linder and Cantrell, 2000; Osterwalder *et al.*, 2005; for a thorough review, please see Morris *et al.*, 2005). For example, Chesbrough and Rosenbloom (2002, p. 550) took a clear starting point in the strategy literature and argued that the business model is offered as a construct that mediates the value creation process as it "translates between the technical and the economic domains, selecting and filtering technologies, and packaging them into particular configurations to be offered to a chosen target market". Although Chesbrough and Rosenbloom's construct clearly relies on a "firm and market" approach, the cases presented exemplify how the companies' business models emerge from interactive processes involving, for example, entrepreneurs, customers and sources of funding.

The business model concept also has intimate connections to the corporate disclosure and communication and transparency perspective as illustrated by Nielsen (2005). With regard to the existing debate on companies' lack of disclosure of relevant information to the investment community, especially when dealing with dynamic, knowledge-intensive and high-growth companies, the critics all too often state that there is an inherent lack of disclosure on non-financial, forward-looking data (Beattie and Pratt, 2002; Eccles and Mavrinac, 1995; Gelb, 2002; Holland, 1997, 2001; Lev, 2001) of the type associated with describing business models. Garten (2001, p. 1) identifies business model descriptions as a major missing piece alongside, for example, market information, operating performance measurements and intellectual capital. Furthermore, business models enable the creation of a comprehensive and more correct set of non-financial value drivers of the company (Kozberg, 2001).

Many efforts are currently under way to support sufficient communication regarding companies' value creation processes. Integrated reporting (see www.iirc.org) is an interesting example of this, as it is essentially reporting – more thoroughly than traditional financial reporting enables – on company strategy, drivers of value creation and intellectual capital: all components relating to a company's business model. As a matter of fact, the business model is at the very core of the International Integrated Reporting Council's (IIRC) framework. This trajectory shows that, from being a buzzword associated with dot-com companies at the turn of the millennium with dubious performance, the term business model has gradually become the new hot management and strategy topic.

As mentioned by DaSilva and Trkman (2014), the number of contributions with 'business model' in their title has remained relatively stable between 2004 and 2007 at 25–42 papers each year. It began to grow again, with 45, 68 and 83 papers, in 2008, 2009 and 2010, respectively. The trend indicates that the 2004–2007 period was characterized by a change in focus from the business model of Internet companies to the analysis of business models in 'general business'.

The business model term quickly spread to the analysis of industries such as airlines (Lawton and Solomko, 2005; Tretheway, 2004), biotechnology (Bigliardi *et al.*, 2005; Nosella *et al.*, 2005), media and telecommunications (Amberg and Schröder, 2007; Eriksson and Kalling, 2007; Ha and Ganahl, 2004) and music (Manafy, 2006; Swatman *et al.*, 2006; for a thorough analysis, see Lambert and Davidson, 2013). Classifying enterprises according to their business models has provided a new perspective to the analysis of young and fast-growing industries or traditional sectors disrupted by technological changes. Business-model-based classifications lend themselves to performing other studies, the aim being to analyze the relationship between homogenous groups of business models and performance (DeYoung, 2005; Flouris and Walker, 2007; Zott and Amit, 2007). This body of research has contributed to the identification of the business model as one of the factors that influence company success in terms of profitability, revenue growth and/or market capitalization.

Also, within the realm of corporate valuation, the business model concept has gradually arisen as one of the main factors to be considered overall concerning the valuation of high-tech companies, such as biotechnology companies. Although the fundamental principles of investment remain the same, whether dealing with a high-tech enterprise or a traditional production company (Fenigstein, 2003), there is often much greater uncertainty regarding high-tech companies' future prospects. Fenigstein (2003, p. 1) highlights that valuation of high-tech companies should be based upon an analysis of "the critical success factors on which a business can survive and succeed", including value drivers such as the business opportunity, the unique value proposition and technology, customer base, competitive advantages and strategic alliances, all of which are elements relating to business models.

Along these lines, Teece (2010) concludes that to be a source of competitive advantage, a business model must be something more than just a good, logical way of doing business. Such a model, he argues, must be honed to meet particular customer needs. It must also be inimitable in certain respects, either by virtue of being difficult to replicate, or by being problematic for competitors to replicate because it would disturb their existing relationships with customers, suppliers or important alliance partners.

In parallel to the body of research focused on the relationship between business models and performance, another relevant stream of research has arisen, concerning business model innovation.

Rising attention on this form of innovation is due to companies' awareness that business models are not static and enduring items. On the contrary, they must be changed, refined and innovated on a systematic basis if companies aim to survive and stay competitive over time.

Over the years, attempts have been made to define when a change can be called business model innovation (Chesbrough, 2007a; Garcia and Calantone, 2002), and several aspects of this phenomenon have been explored: drivers of business model innovation (de Reuver *et al.*, 2009; Moyon and Lecocq, 2010), features of the process of business model innovation (Dunford, 2010; McGrath, 2010), tools to support the process of business model innovation (Gnatzy and Moser, 2012; Hienerth *et al.*, 2011), and levers to successful business model innovation (Giesen *et al.*, 2010; Sosna *et al.*, 2010).

Following this, Nunes and Breene (2011) argue that companies successfully reinventing themselves have in common the ability to broaden their focus beyond what they denote "the financial S curve" where the profitability of a product or service will decline over time as competition rises in the product lifecycle. Rather, they argue that companies should focus on managing three much shorter but vitally important "hidden S curves": (1) tracking the basis of competition in the industry;

(2) renewal of the capabilities in the organization; and (3) nurturing a ready supply of talent. In essence, this means that managers should constantly focus on fixing what does not yet appear to be broken.

The literature has also been rich with frameworks and ontologies for conceptualizing the potential concept of what's in and what's out of a business model analysis, as well as representing and explaining relationships among business model components. One such example is Richardson's (2008) framework that integrates business models with the concept of strategy execution. His framework addresses the notions of value proposition, value creation and delivery system, and value capture. Richardson's (2008, p. 138) Business Model Framework is as follows:

- The value proposition – what the firm will deliver to its customers, why they will be willing to pay for it, and the firm's basic approach to competitive advantage
  - a The offering
  - b The target customer
  - c The basic strategy to win customers and gain competitive advantage
- The value creation and delivery system – how the firm will create and deliver that value to its customers and the source of its competitive advantage
  - a Resources and capabilities
  - b Organization: the value chain, activity system and business processes
  - c Position in the value network: links to suppliers, partners, and customers
- Value capture – how the firm generates revenue and profit
  - a Revenue sources
  - b The economics of the business

Figure 2 provides a timeline diagram that summarizes the most popular drivers of the business model concept over time. Interestingly, the popularity of the business model can in part also be attributed to research articles on business models outside the business sphere (DaSilva and Trkman, 2014), and the term has been used in a variety of different scientific disciplines in recent years:

- Political parties such as the Labour Party in the UK (Faucher-King, 2008);
- Terrorist organizations such as Al-Qaeda (Vardi, 2010);

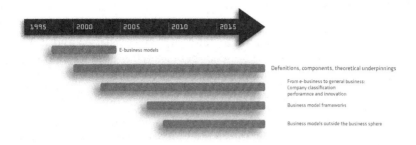

Figure 2 Popularity drivers of the business model concept over time.

- Environmental conservation (Sovinc, 2009);
- The model of the US economy (Cappelli, 2009);
- Any kind of human endeavour with a wide range of interpretations (Ghaziani and Ventresca, 2005); and
- The development of rare diseases (Ferry, 2010).

Whether dealing with innovation, entrepreneurship, organizational change or strategy and so forth, the general argument that can be developed from the earlier sections is that the business model perspective holds an advantageous starting point for creating a comprehensive and mutual understanding of how a company creates value. However, as will be evident from the following review, although there are numerous attempts at defining what a business model is, a clear definition remains elusive.

Recent developments in business model research

The term business model suggests a sophisticated and structured approach to business, one that is at the heart of business success. It suggests that a recipe for success can be taken from an organization – such as Apple, Amazon, Facebook or Twitter – and applied to other organizations, bringing similar success. However, each of these companies has achieved success in different ways, and there is no one size fits all business model – the field is more complex and nuanced than that. Thus, academics and practitioners ask, "What is a business model?", and "How can companies develop their own successful business model?" These big questions are still unanswered in business model research and practice.

From its origin more than 60 years ago, the concept of the business model (Bellman *et al.*, 1957), has developed through what Wirtz *et al.*

(2016b) call the "formation phase" of business model research in the 1990s. From a practitioner perspective, a negative association with the term business model developed around the same time due to the involvement of e-businesses in the dot-com bubble (Nielsen and Bukh, 2011). Since the end of the dot-com bubble, Wirtz *et al.* (2016b) have identified a "differentiation phase", incorporating an increase in practice-oriented articles and books, as well as several special issues in leading academic journals, such as *Long Range Planning*[1] and the *Harvard Business Review.*[2] Research into business models continues to thrive, with a surge in conference tracks at well-established academic conferences and the advent of the Business Model Community, with over 400 members.[3] This increase in attention may be due to practitioners' increasing perception of the relevance of business models, which is seeing growth in the use of business model terminology and frameworks in relation to business development (Johnson *et al.*, 2008), management (Arend, 2013) and entrepreneurship (Certo *et al.*, 2009; Doganova and Eyquem-Renault, 2009).

One notable framework is Osterwalder and Pigneur's (2010) Business Model Canvas, presented in their book *Business Model Generation*, which to date has sold more than 1.3 million copies and has been translated into over 30 languages. Additionally, there are now several dedicated journals in the field, such as *Journal of Business Models* and *Open Journal of Business Model Innovation* that provide an opportunity for the exploration of new research contributions. The field of business model research is both vibrant and progressive.

For example, the *Journal of Business Models* has recently published contributions that analyze business models from several, new perspectives, such as scalability (Lund and Nielsen, 2018), ecosystems (D'Souza *et al.*, 2015; Iivari *et al.*, 2016), performance measurement (Heikkilä *et al.*, 2014) or accounting (Haslam *et al.*, 2013). Business models have also been investigated within particular contexts, like small to medium-sized enterprises (Iivari, 2015; Schüle *et al.*, 2016), networks (Hakanen *et al.*, 2016; Lund and Nielsen, 2014) or born global firms (Johansson and Abrahamsson, 2016).

Moreover, business model innovation has been explored from different angles: for example, the market-driven perspective (Zalewska-Kurek *et al.*, 2016), the patterns perspective (Lüttgens and Diener, 2016), the portfolio strategy perspective (Verhoeven and Johnson, 2016) or the risk management perspective (Taran *et al.*, 2013).

In addition, the investigation of business models' theoretical underpinnings has progressed. For example, Foss and Saebi (2017) use complexity theory to analyze the business model concept from a theoretical perspective. On the one hand, this entails conceptualizing the business model as a set of interdependent and complementary subsystems that interact in a complex way; on the other hand, this lends itself to identifying different types of business models (highly modular, non-decomposable, nearly decomposable), according to the degree of interdependency among subsystems, and, therefore, different types of business model innovation.

Business model research is also prominent in fields outside of business and management, such as practical entrepreneurship (Osterwalder *et al.*, 2014), production and technology (Bocken *et al.*, 2014), sustainability (Prahalad and Hart, 2002) and software development (O'Reilly, 2007). Research in these fields generally reviews and discusses definitions, concepts and frameworks for describing and developing business models from different perspectives, such as Timmers' (1998) review of business model for e-business. These domain-specific reviews are typically motivated by an interest in examination of a specific field and do not necessarily take a broad approach to the business model concept, conveying only a partial picture of the business model field. For example, the business model definitions used in these papers are often narrow and overlook the complexity of the business model (Hedman and Kalling, 2003; Mahadevan, 2000; Timmers, 1998), while the studies in these papers are frequently authorship reviews based on subjective interpretations, rather than on empirically structured approaches (Massaro *et al.*, 2016a). Shafer *et al.* (2005, p. 199) argue that "while it has become quite fashionable to discuss business models, there is still much confusion about what business models are and how they can be used".

To counter these limitations in the field of business model research, contributions published in the differentiation phase, as outlined by Wirtz *et al.* (2016b), tend to be more structured in a search for the common elements of a business model. For example, Schafer *et al.* (2005) uncovered 12 different business model definitions between 1998 and 2002 to create their own definition: a business model is a "representation of a firm's underlying core logic and strategic choices for creating and capturing value within a value network" (p. 202). Osterwalder *et al.* (2005, p. 33), in relation to the working information systems domain, argue that

> one of the shortcomings in the business model literature is that the different authors rarely build on each other's work. Consequently, business model research as a whole, advances more slowly than it could and often stays at a superficial level.

Following along these lines, Teece (2010, p. 192) states:

> The paucity of literature (both theoretical and practical) on the topic is remarkable, given the importance of business design, particularly in the context of innovation. The economics literature has failed to even flag the importance of the phenomenon, in part because of an implicit assumption that markets are perfect or very nearly so. The strategy and organization literature has done little better. Like other interdisciplinary topics, business models are frequently mentioned but rarely analyzed: therefore, they are often poorly understood. Not surprisingly, it is common to see great technological achievements fail commercially because little, if any, attention has been given to designing a business model to take them to market properly.

Zott *et al.* (2011) set out to uncover contemporary developments and future research by providing a comprehensive literature review on the business model. They also identify the absence of a generally accepted idea of what a business model is and concluded that contemporary research is evolving into silos based on "(1) e-business and the use of information technology in organizations; (2) strategic issues, such as value creation, competitive advantage, and firm performance; and (3) innovation and technology management" (p. 1020).

Similarly, Wirtz *et al.* (2016a, 2016b) examine the current state of business model research using a "synoptic literature analysis". They identify four essential research areas: innovation, change and evolution, performance and controlling and design. However, their review is based on an initial subjective analysis, and while the authors confirm these research foci with a panel of experts, the areas identified are general concepts rather than outlines of specific research questions.

As the previous sections have shown, the business model is a very heterogeneous research area that over time has developed in several, different directions, drawing on a multitude of management disciplines, including entrepreneurship, strategy, organization, information systems and innovation. The lack of constructs clarity and the uncertainty of the theoretical underpinnings prevent the process of cumulative growth of knowledge as different authors rarely build on each other's work, making research efforts disconnected and characterized by conceptual ambiguity.

By nature, previous domain specific and non-structured reviews can only partially solve this problem. This situation demands a structured and comprehensive analysis that assesses and evaluates the current state of research on business models, identifies the experts in this research area, pinpoints the methodologies used in previous studies and highlights key questions, research gaps and areas that deserve additional attention, with the aim to establish a sound foundation for future research.

Notes

1 2010, Volume 43, Issues 2/3.
2 For example, December 2008 and January–February 2011.
3 see www.businessmodelcommunity.com.

2 Applied research methodology

This chapter uses a structured literature review (SLR) methodology "to develop insights, critical reflections, future research paths and research questions" for the field of business model research (Massaro et al., 2016a, p. 767). The SLR methodology potentially offers less bias and more transparency because it relies on a set of rules that underpin validation and reliability. Given that business model research to date lacks specific research questions needed to drive future research, the SLR methodology is ideally suited to building on the work of Zott et al. (2011) and Wirtz et al. (2016b).

According to Hart (1998, p. 1) a literature reviews allow understanding of a topic, focusing on "what has already been done on it, how it has been researched, and what the key issues are". Massaro et al. (2016a, p. 767) outline that there are several different literature review methodologies, and the SLR is a methodology "for studying a corpus of scholarly literature, to develop insights, critical reflections, future research paths and research questions". Therefore, we use the SLR methodology to develop a "systematic, objective, replicable and reliable process" (Massaro et al., 2016a, p. 767).

In developing a literature review, researchers "should adopt a questioning and critical attitude" (Hart, 1998, p. 30). Alveson and Deetz (2000) highlight that there are three tasks of critical management research – insight, critique and transformative redefinitions – and following these, we develope three research questions (RQs) for this book.

RQ1: Insights. How is the field of business model developing?
RQ2: Critique. What is the critique of business model research?
RQ3: Transformative redefinitions. What are the likely future scenarios for business model research?

In developing our review and critique, we design our research in line with a number of other recent contributions critically investigating business model research (Arend, 2013; Baden-Fuller and Mangematin, 2013; Jensen, 2014). The research for this article begins with the data set used in Zott *et al.* (2011) and expands it to include publications from a wider range of information sources that go beyond academic articles from selected outlets. Consistent with Massaro *et al.* (2016b), to help understand the impact of publications in the field of business models, we supplement the data set by including citation data from Google Scholar and thereby develop a publication impact analysis that is presented in the following subsection (Dumay, 2014).

Publication impact

Citation counts are becoming a shared measure for identifying the impact of scientific publications and can be used to analyze how specific topics evolve over time (Massaro *et al.*, 2016a, pp. 780–781). Each publication selected for this study was measured using Google Scholar Citations (GSC), citations per year (CPY) and the last five years (CI5Y). Initially, 365 cited sources were found on Google Scholar using the search term "business model*". This meant that the search captured sources using terminologies such as business model, business models and business modelling. Next, we constructed three league tables of the top 100 sources according to the three criteria: GSC, CPY and CI5Y. From these league tables, we identified the 79 publications that appear in all three top-100 tables. These 79 publications thereby represent the most impactful work in the field of business models.

Defining the analytical framework

In developing a SLR, it must be decided "what is to be observed as well as how observations are to be recorded and thereafter considered data" (Krippendorff, 2013). The first level of our analytical framework focuses on the 'when' dimension. Papers are analyzed considering their evolution over time, both in terms of number of papers and number of citations. The second level focuses on the 'who' dimensions. Author demographics are recorded focusing on the number of publications by each author and the background of the first author. Furthermore, we distinguish between academics and non-academics. The objective here is to analyze who are the most prominent authors in the field, as well as to understand the role of practitioners. The third and fourth levels of analysis focus on the 'what' and 'how' dimensions respectively, studying the research questions and the research methods used to gain an understanding of the scientific maturity of the field. The last level of analysis focuses on the 'which' dimension, or main implications, distinguishing between practical and research definitions.

The categories in Table 1 were designed to answer RQ1 concerning how the field of business models has been developing on an overall level. The analysis of these questions is furthermore expected to lead to insights that generate critique of the field (RQ2) and also to a transformative redefinition (RQ3).

Table 1 Dimensions of the structured literature review

Level	Description	Details	Total results	%	Krippendorff's alpha
When.	Article evolution over time				
	Years		**80**	**100**	**1.000**
	<= 2000		13	16	
	2001–2005		33	41	
	2006–2010		31	39	
	2011–2015		3	14	
Who.	Author demographics				
	All authors		**144**	**100**	**1.000**
	N. of authors with more than one publication		15	10	
	of which among the top cited	*9*		*64*	
	First author		**80**	**100**	**1.000**
	Non-Academic		9	11	
	Junior Academic		25	31	
	Professor		46	58	
Where.	Country of origin and publication outlet				
	Country of origin*		**80**	**100**	
	Not applicable		60	75	
	Europe		13	16	
	England	*1*		*1*	
	Finland	*1*		*1*	
	France	*2*		*3*	
	Germany	*2*		*3*	
	Italy	*1*		*1*	
	Norway	*1*		*1*	
	Spain	*1*		*1*	
	Switzerland	*2*		*3*	
	The Netherlands	*1*		*1*	

Level	Description	Details	Total results	%	Krippendorff's alpha
	North America		10	13	
	United States	*10*		*13*	
	Asia		2	3	
	Bangladesh	*1*		*1*	
	India	*1*		*1*	
	Oceania		1	1	
	Australia	*1*		*1*	
	Publication outlet		**80**	**100**	**1.000**
	Long-range Planning		13	15	
	Harvard Business School Press.		6	8	
	Harvard Business Review		4	5	
	Strategic Management Journal		4	5	
	European Journal of Information Systems		3	4	
	MIT Sloan Management Review		3	4	
	Organization Science		3	4	
	Academy of Management Perspectives		2	3	
	Electronic Markets		2	3	
	Journal of Management		2	3	
	Journal of Marketing		2	3	
	Management Decision		2	3	
	Management Science		2	3	
	McGraw-Hill		2	3	
	Research Policy		2	3	
	Others (only one article per outlet)		28	35	

What. Business model definition and research themes

Level	Description	Details	Total results	%	Krippendorff's alpha
	Business model definition		**80**	**100**	**0.974**
	Provide a business model definition		47	59	
	Does not provide a business model definition		33	41	

How. Research questions and research methods

Level	Description	Details	Total results	%	Krippendorff's alpha
	Research questions		**80**	**100**	**0.974**
	Provide a research question		31	39	
	Does not provide a research question		49	61	
	Main research questions provided*		**31**	**100**	**Not applicable***

(*Continued*)

Level	Description	Details	Total results	%	Krippendorff's alpha
	What's the definition of business model?		7	23	
	How does business model evolve?		4	13	
	How can business model be implemented and used?		8	26	
	How can the business model support innovation?		2	6	
	What are the barriers to business model implementation?		1	3	
	How does business model interact with managerial cognition and action?		2	6	
	How does business model affect performance?		8	26	
	What are emerging business models?		2	6	
	Which are the strategies implemented in new business models?		2	6	
	What are the factors affecting business model adoption?		4	13	
	Applied research methods*		**80**	**100**	**1.000**
	Literature review		11	14	
	Conceptual Article		48	60	
	Survey, Questionnaire		4	5	
	Panel Data or Similar Quantitative Study		1	1	
	Case Study (Non-Intervention)		12	15	
	Action Research (Intervention Research)		0	0	
	Mixed Methods		4	5	

Which implications. Practical and research implications

Level	Description	Details	Total results	%	Krippendorff's alpha
	Practical implications		**80**	**100**	**1.000**
	Reports practical implications		25	31	
	Does not report practical implications		55	69	
	Research implications		**80**	**100**	**1.000**
	Reports research implications		28	35	
	Does not report research implications		52	65	

Developing reliability

The coding was done by two researchers. First, three publications were coded independently by reading them and recording the codes onto separate spreadsheets. Notes were compared and major coding discrepancies were discussed as well as issues relating to jurisdiction. This process was repeated until the reliability of the results was satisfactory. Additionally, the authors performed a Krippendorff's alpha test to assure coding reliability (Krippendorff, 2013).

Testing literature review validity

External validity of this type of content analysis is aimed at establishing whether the results of a study can be generalized. In this study, the authors performed queries in the EBSCO database, as well as through Google Scholar and existing literature reviews containing data on publications, to confirm whether the selected works were representative of the literature. Among these literature reviews was Zott *et al.* (2011). Two researchers read the abstracts of identified papers, and in some cases the full paper, to establish their relevance. Publications that were discarded as being within the scope of this research typically did not have the theme of business models as a substantive subject matter, but rather used the term superficially in relation to another discipline.

Publication coding

After defining the analytical framework and checking the framework's reliability as described earlier, one researcher coded the remainder of the works. Reliability checking and discussion of codes where there was uncertainty was carried out continuously throughout the process by the authors.

3   Insights

How the field of business models is developing

This section answers the first research question: "How is the field of business models developing?" Table 1 depicts the results of this analysis, while the following subsections discuss the main findings.

When: paper evolution over time

Focusing on the 'when' dimension, Figure 1 summarizes the results according to total citation by year to identify trends in citation patterns. Results show that most of the citations on the topic are concentrated around the period 2001–2003 with two further citation spikes in 2007 and 2010. It is worth noting that of the contributions published in the period 2001–2003, eight publications out of 20 have received more than 1,000 citations, with six publications having a CPY in excess of 100. From the 2007 citation spike, only two of seven of the published works have received more than 1,000 citations to date, and only these two contributions have a CPY of over 100. Similarly, only two of 14 of the works published from 2010 and onwards have more than 1,000 citations and show a CPY over 100. These results indicate that the business model literature may already have reached maturity in the period 2001–2003, with some important innovations to the field being published in 2007 and 2010. Figure 3 indicates that there is a distinct set of stages in business model research. Axes on the left and right measure total citations and CPY of contributions published for each year.

The first citation spike revealed in the data relates to the period 2001–2003. This citation spike is driven by several authors, all of whom were well known in their respective fields prior to their business model publication. The contributions primarily relate to the definition of business models and especially how they differ from strategy (Hamel, 2000; Magretta, 2002; Porter, 2001). Several papers that describe early conceptual models and typologies depicting the possible content of a

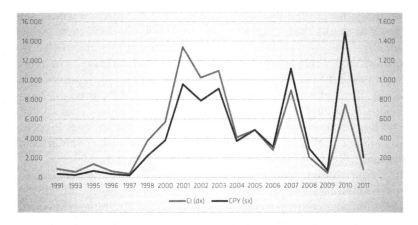

Figure 3 Citation index (CI) and citation per year index (CPY) of published articles.

business model are likewise present in this citation spike, for example, Chesbrough and Rosenbloom (2002). A dominant sub-theme among the works published during this first spike is the e-business perspective, which is typically closely linked to developing either conceptual models, typologies or business model definitions.

The second citation spike, in 2007, relates mainly to publications about innovating business models. The most cited work, O'Reilley (2007), argues that successful business model patterns create value in the Web 2.0 context, also called social media. It is also worth noting that Teece's (2007) article discussing dynamic capabilities, is an important seminal contribution aimed at theorising business models.

The third citation spike occurs in 2010. The primary driver here is Osterwalder and Pigneur's (2010) book about the Business Model Canvas. This spike is also driven by the special issue of *Long Range Planning* that includes several of the dominant authors already present in the first spike of citations described earlier. It is interesting to note that all three citation spikes are driven both by practitioner and academic insights, but where the academic literature is more dispersed across the whole period of study, the practitioner insights are more concentrated around these spikes.

Who: author demographics

The second measure depicted in the analytical framework focuses on author demographics. The results show that 148 authors are responsible for publishing the 79 works analyzed. Only 15 authors published more than one work, and of these 15, nine are within the top cited works that reached more than 1,000 citations each. Additionally, focusing on those top cited publications, 77% are written by authors who wrote more than one piece in this category. The most prominent authors are Henry Chesbrough, who has co-authored six works, three of which are among the most cited (Chesbrough, 2003, 2006; Chesbrough and Rosenbloom, 2002), Alexander Osterwalder, who has co-authored four works, of which three with Yves Pigneur are among the most cited (Osterwalder, 2004; Osterwalder and Pigneur, 2010; Osterwalder *et al.*, 2005), and Prahalad and Teece, who have co-authored two works, each among the most cited (Prahalad and Hammond, 2002; Prahalad and Hart, 2002; Teece, 2007, 2010). These findings confirm trends found in different disciplines (Massaro *et al.*, 2015, 2016b), where prominent authors attract more citations and gain greater recognition in the field.

Studying the work of the prominent authors within the field demonstrates that these authors take a narrow focus; that is, they specialize in an aspect of the field. For example, Henry Chesbrough's focus is open innovation in a business model context, David Teece depicts the business model relationship to strategy, and Alex Osterwalder and Yves Pigneur develop their framework that eventually becomes the Business Model Canvas in 2010. Table 2 reports the top cited publications.

Additionally, focusing on the distribution of the first author of the publications, results show that 11% of the publications have a non-academic first author. By cross-matching with the number of citations, our results show that the non-academic works published in the spike periods 2007 and 2010 account for 45% and 28% of all citations. While the non-academics were not drivers of the citation development of the first studies on business models in the period 2001–2003, they largely contribute to the development of the following spikes in 2007 and 2010. Thus, while both practitioners and academics contribute to the first development of the research field at the end of the 1990s, the topic was largely dominated by academics until the two more recent spikes in 2007 and 2010. Figure 4 depicts these results.

Where: author origins and publication outlets

Analyzing the first author's geographic origin, results show that most of the relevant studies have been published in the US and in the UK. In continental Europe, Spain and France are the most prolific countries.

Table 2 Top cited articles

Article	Author	Year	No. of citations	Source
Open innovation – The new imperative for creating and profiting from technology	Chesbrough, Henry W.	2003	9227	Harvard Business School Press
Strategy and the internet	Porter, Michael E.	2001	4920	Harvard Business Review
The fortune at the bottom of the pyramid	Prahalad, C.K.; Hart, Stuart L.	2002	4088	Strategy + Business
What is Web 2.0: design patterns and business models for the next generation of software	O'Reilly, T.	2007	3991	Communications & Strategies
Value creation in e-business	Amit, Raphael; Zott, Christoph	2001	3304	Strategic Management Journal
Explicating dynamic capabilities: the nature and microfoundations of (sustainable) enterprise performance	Teece, David J.	2007	3021	Strategic Management Journal
Leading the revolution	Hamel, G.	2000	2727	Harvard Business School Press
Business models for electronic markets	Timmers, P.	1998	2354	Electronic Markets
The role of the business model in capturing value from innovation: evidence from Xerox Corporation's technology spin-off companies	Chesbrough, Henry; Rosenbloom, Richard S.	2002	2154	Industrial and Corporate Change
Business Model Generation: A Handbook for Visionaries, Game Changers, and Challengers	Osterwalder, Alexander; Pigneur, Yves	2010	2097	John Wiley & Sons
Why business models matter	Magretta, Joan	2002	1842	Harvard Business Review
Open Business Models: How to Thrive in the New Innovation Landscape	Chesbrough, Henry W.	2006	1750	Harvard Business School Press
Internet business models and strategies: Text and cases	Afuah, A; Tucci, C.L.	2004	1552	McGraw-Hill

(Continued)

Article	Author	Year	No. of citations	Source
Configuring value for competitive advantage: on chains, shops, and networks	Stabell, Charles B.; Fjeldstad, Øystein D.	1998	1387	Strategic Management Journal
Shifting paradigms for sustainable development – implications for management theory and research	Gladwin, Thomas N.; Kennelly, James J.; Krause, Tara-Shelomith	1995	1376	Academy of Management Review
Business models, business strategy and innovation	Teece, David J.	2010	1368	Long Range Planning
Clarifying business models: origins, present, and future of the concept	Osterwalder, Alexander; Pigneur, Yves; Tucci, Christopher	2005	1302	Communications of the Association for Information Systems
Serving the world's poor, profitably	Prahalad, C.K.; Hammond, Allen	2002	1206	Harvard Business Review
The business model ontology – a proposition in a design science approach	Osterwalder, Alexander	2004	1169	Dissertation, University of Lausanne
Digital capital: Harnessing the Power of Business Webs	Tapscott, D.; Lowy, A.; Ticoll, D.	2001	1094	Harvard Business School Press
The entrepreneur's business model: toward a unified perspective	Morris, Michael; Schindehutte, Minet; Allen, Jeffrey	2005	1093	Journal of Business Research

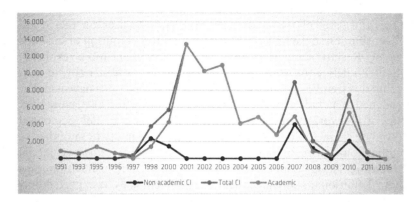

Figure 4 Citation index (CI) between non-academics, academics and total.

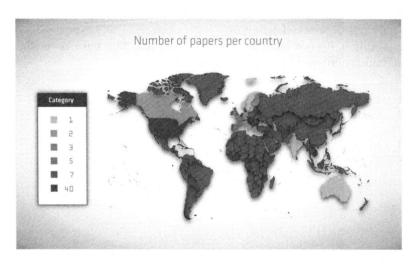

Figure 5 First author country of origin.

Interestingly, there are no relevant studies published in any emerging countries such as China, South America or any African country. Figure 5 depicts these results.

Similar results can be gained focusing on the publication outlet. Most of the outlets where prominent articles have been published are from the US with *Long Range Planning*, *Harvard Business Review* and *Strategic Management Journal* that together account for more than 33% of all the papers published in the field.

What: business model definition and research themes

The third level of the analytical framework focuses on the 'what' dimension. First, we look at papers that apply a definition of business model. Results show that only 58% of the publications explicitly (46 of 79) define the concept of business model. Additionally, in analyzing this trend over time, the more recent publications have a higher tendency to include a business model definition. After 2005, more than 60% of the works provide a definition of business model, compared to only 37% in the previous period. Figure 6 depicts the number of publications (absolute and percentage) that provide a business model definition. These results confirm Zott *et al.*'s (2011, p. 1034) findings that "definitional and conceptual disagreement is to be expected during the emergent phase of any new potentially big idea of general usefulness". The evolution of different definitions is forcing authors to clarify the definition they apply (Jensen, 2014). However, despite the growing trend, almost 40% of the recent publications still do not provide a business model definition.

Additionally, our empirical analysis illustrates that business model definitions fall into five overall categories:

1   Logic and value chain;
2   Components and structure;
3   Value and value proposition;
4   Market and customers; and
5   Processes.

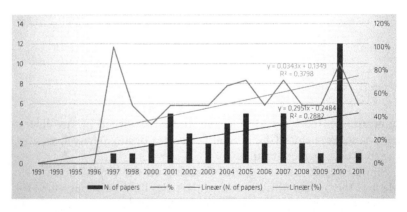

Figure 6 Development of business model definition inclusion over time.

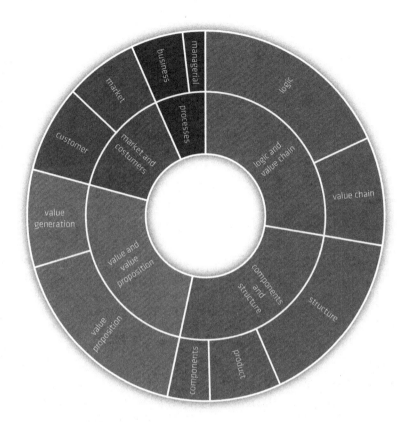

Figure 7 Business model definitions.

Figure 7 shows that each of these categories consists of a number of subcategories.

Focusing on research themes, the results show that some topics are recent. For example, business model innovation has 80% of the articles after 2005, while encompassing boundary spanning activities and strategic partners has six of seven papers after 2005. Other topics are declining. For example, the connection with value creation has only one paper after 2005. Additionally, there are no links to the impact in terms of policymakers. Figure 8 depicts these results.

Interestingly, some topics are country-centred. Definitions are addressed from either Switzerland or the US, whereas for example, several themes are highly US based: sustainability (four papers out of

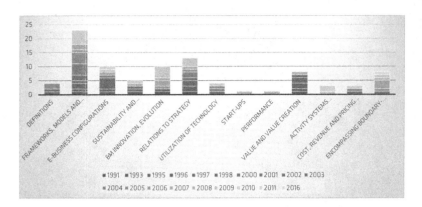

Figure 8 Business model themes and their evolution over time.

five), strategy (seven out of thirteen), technology (three out of four); and value creation (six out of eight). Other themes are more balanced. For example, frameworks are proposed in Europe, the US and Australia, as well as e-business focused papers. Additionally, analyzing the different type of authors, we can see that junior academics are more focused on frameworks and definitions. Table 3 depicts these results.

How: research questions and research methods

The fourth level of the analytical framework also focuses on the 'how' dimension. Results show that only 38% of the analyzed publications (30 out of 79) specifically present one or more research questions. Publications with one or more research questions are generally published more recently and the percentage of publications that state research questions increases over time. According to Zott *et al.* (2011, p. 1020), "it appears that researchers (and practitioners) have yet to develop a common and widely accepted language that would allow researchers who examine the business model construct through different lenses to draw effectively on the work of others". This might in part explain the lack of idea-sharing among the dominant authors as highlighted earlier in the 'who' section. Massaro *et al.* (2016a, p. 273) suggest that "understanding if and how the articles analyzed provide specific research questions could help in understanding the evolution of the research topic". Therefore, the use of a research question can help to increase the transparency (Ketokivi and Choi, 2014) of research and may be seen as a sign of the field's scientific maturity (Massaro *et al.*, 2015).

Table 3 Theme and country of the first author

Country	Definitions	Creating frameworks, models and techniques	E-business configurations	Sustainability and socially oriented business models	Business model innovation, Evolution	Relations to strategy	Utilisation of technology	Start-ups	Performance	Value; value creation	Activity systems perspective	Cost, revenue architectures and pricing mechanisms	Encompassing boundary-spanning activities and strategic partners	Total
Greece	–	1	–	–	–	–	–	–	–	–	–	–	–	1
US	2	8	4	4	5	7	3	–	–	6	–	1	4	44
UK	–	3	–	–	1	1	–	–	–	1	1	–	1	8
Finland	–	2	–	–	–	–	–	–	–	–	–	–	–	2
France	–	–	–	–	1	2	–	1	1	–	–	–	1	6
Spain	–	1	1	–	1	1	–	–	–	–	2	1	–	7
Switzerland	2	4	–	–	1	–	–	–	–	–	–	–	–	7
Belgium	–	–	1	–	–	–	–	–	–	–	–	–	–	1
India	–	–	1	–	–	–	–	–	–	–	–	–	–	1
Italy	–	–	–	–	–	1	1	–	–	–	–	–	–	2
Norway	–	–	–	–	–	–	–	–	–	1	–	–	–	1
Netherlands	–	–	1	–	1	–	–	–	–	–	–	1	1	4
Austria	–	1	–	–	–	–	–	–	–	–	–	–	–	1
Canada	–	–	1	1	–	1	–	–	–	–	–	–	–	3
Australia	–	1	–	–	–	–	–	–	–	–	–	–	–	1
Germany	–	1	1	–	–	–	–	–	–	–	–	–	1	3
Sweden	–	1	–	–	–	–	–	–	–	–	–	–	–	1
Total	**4**	**23**	**10**	**5**	**10**	**13**	**4**	**1**	**1**	**8**	**3**	**3**	**8**	**93**

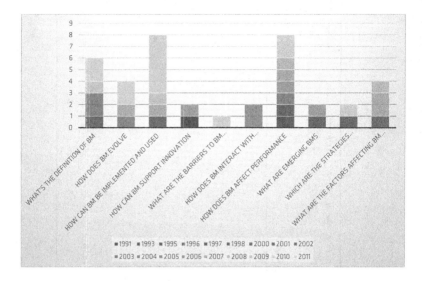

Figure 9 Types of research questions and their evolution over time (darker is older while lighter is more recent).

Our analyses (Figure 9) shows that the most important research questions (eight works each) relate to the impact of the business model on performance and the implementation of business models. For example, Zott and Amit (2007, p. 182) specifically ask "how business model design can be measured, and how it affects firm performance". Interestingly, the definition of business model and its evolution, such as the factors affecting business model adoption, is a research question in 14 publications. For example, Al-Debei and Avison (2010, p. 360) address the following issue: "The dimensions and elements of the business model concept, that is, what constitutes business models, or what aspects need examining when designing, evaluating, and managing business models". Other research questions are related to the barriers to implementation (e.g. Chesbrough, 2010) and innovation of business models, such as the strategic approach to the business model and the definition of the emerging business model. Even though papers with research questions are published more frequently, the results show that the dispersion over time differs significantly. Some research questions, such as "how to implement business models", occur more frequently in recent contributions, while other research questions, such as the impact of business models on performance, are more equally distributed across time.

Next, our study analyses the research methods applied in each of the contributions. Our findings (Figure 10) show that 60% of the

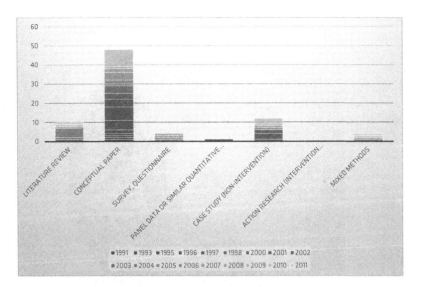

Figure 10 Research method, evolution over time (darker is older while lighter is more recent).

publications (48 of 79) are conceptual in nature. Empirical studies represent 27% of the studies (21 of 79), while literature reviews represent 12% of the studies (10 of 79). This is quite similar to the results presented by Wirtz *et al.* (2016b), although that study does not consider the impact of the identified works. Analyzing the methods used over time, we find that conceptual contributions are fairly evenly distributed over the period of analysis, although there is a concentration of papers published in the period 2000–2003 (19 papers), in 2007 (4 papers) and in 2010 (9 papers). Empirical contributions represent a minority of papers (only 25 papers) and are more recently published, with 14 of 25 papers published after 2007. Interestingly, six of the 15 literature reviews were published in the period 2000–2003, while seven literature reviews were published after 2010. Finally, citation trends show that conceptual work attracts considerably more citations compared to other contributions, since 60% of these publications garner 74% of the total citations.

Which implications: practical and research implications

The final level of the analytical framework focuses on practical and research implications. The results show that only 13% (or 10) of the publications analyzed specifically report practical implications. Figure 11 reports most common practical implications.

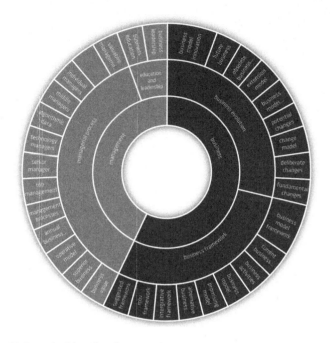

Figure 11 Practical implications.

For example, Dubosson-Torbay *et al.* (2002, p. 22) state "the outcomes of this article should help the managers design a new business model by using the suggested framework and by which, asking the right questions, such as what is exactly my value proposition". Similarly, Demil and Lecocq (2010, p. 242) state that their "framework may constitute a useful artifact to help them [the managers] reflect on the design of their business model and how to change it". Implications analyzed refer to the need for understanding the components of the business model and how to integrate them into the company. One example of this is Chesbrough (2007a, p. 17), who states that "a promising model will have to be scaled up, and integrated across the company". Finally, 10 publications discuss the implications of their results for innovating the current business model. For example, Chesbrough (2010, p. 362) states

> at the same time, the organization's culture must find ways to embrace the new model, while maintaining the effectiveness of the current business model until the new one is ready to take over

completely. Only in this way can business model innovation help companies escape the 'trap' of their earlier business models, and renew growth and profits.

Managerial implications are discussed by 12 publications, of which 10 focus on the managerial process. For example, Linder and Cantrell (2000, p. 14) discuss the implications for well-established business practices, such as the development of business plans and state "the days of comprehensive annual business plans that actually stick are over". Other studies focus on the implementation of changed organizational routines. For example, Wirtz *et al.* (2010, p. 287) state "finally, after successfully identifying important trends in their markets and redesigning their business model components accordingly, managers need to implement their new structure and establish modified organizational routines that best address the new environmental landscape".

The two remaining contributions focus on leadership and educational implications. For example, Prahalad and Hart (2002, p. 12) state "it is imperative, however, that managers recognize the nature of business leadership required" while Tikkanen *et al.* (2005, p. 805) state "the business model framework has proven to be a useful tool in business education". Therefore, the main implications have a corporate focus, encompassing implications for the business framework and its evolution and on managerial practices and leadership. None of the studies focused on implications for policymakers.

Focusing on the research implications, results show that only 34% of the publications explicitly discuss research implications and these are dispersed across three main areas of analysis. Figure 12 depicts the main research implications.

The most prominent implication for research in business models relates to scholars proposing research opportunities that focus on the connections between business models and strategy, entrepreneurship, and organizational aspects. For example, Zott and Amit (2010, p. 224) state

an activity systems perspective on business models encourages the incorporation of those ideas, and thus promotes a synthesis of theoretical perspectives ... For example ... how activities are produced by organizational actors drawing on various resources – that is ... the social aspects of relationships between business model participants, as well as the transactional dimension of their relationships.

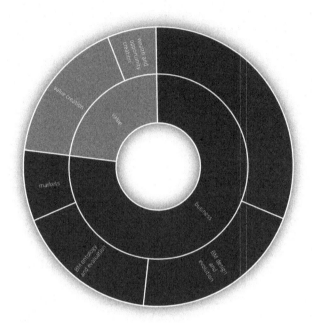

Figure 12 Research implications.

Similarly, Al-Debei and Avison (2010, p. 373) state

> Although we have provided theoretical insights concerning the role of the business model in providing the needed fit between the business strategy and IS [Information System] within digital organizations, there is still a need for future research in this particular area.

The need to better understand how business models evolve is recognized by eight studies. For example, Yunus *et al.* (2010, p. 789) state "The article proposes that the business model can be scrutinized in future studies, especially from the viewpoints of cognition, thus creating new avenues for intra-firm evolutionary studies". Similarly, Zott and Amit (2007, p. 195) recognize new research opportunities in understanding "what factors give rise to and shape business model designs". Finally, specific attention is paid to the relationship between business models and market structures. For example, Mahadevan (2000, p. 68) states "A deeper empirical understanding of the relationship between the market structure and the choice of the business model can be investigated by specific case studies". Therefore, an important research implication for the business model literature is connected with the need to develop and test business model ontologies that can support their design and evolution over time, with specific attention to the market implications and its connection with strategy, entrepreneurship and other organizational aspects, such as existing routines.

Another important research implication connects to value creation and opportunity creation. This is recognized by seven works. More precisely, Jacobides *et al.* (2006, p. 1217) state

> we hope to stimulate further research by reformulating some basic questions, e.g. shifting the question from how do you protect innovation in order to reap the maximum amount of surplus to, how can you find a way to generate value and capture the greatest possible amount of surplus, regardless of whether others emulate the ideas or not.

Similarly, Stabell and Fjeldstad (1998, p. 435) suggest "there are perhaps equally interesting challenges in considering the implications at the business value system level", thus indicating that value creation, and opportunity creation might be related to systems that are broader than the single firm. That is, business models have been recognized in the literature at the ecosystem level but may also be considered from the perspective of broader social consequences.

4 Critique and transformative redefinition

This section answers the second research question: "What is the critique of business model research?" According to Alvesson and Deetz (2000, p. 44), critique revolves around the analysis of dominating messages, structures and power relations; therefore, critique is not a negative concept. Additionally, the development of critical insight is all about the art of interpretation to produce new meanings (Alvesson and Deetz, 2000, p. 44). These are presented in the following subsections.

Critique 1. Author and outlet specialization and practitioners' involvement

The findings show that only a few authors have a high specialization and have produced more than one ranked publication. Our findings show that these specialized authors attract more citations. In other disciplines, such as knowledge management, author distribution has been attributed to the high number of practitioners involved, and Serenko *et al.* (2010, p. 18) state that "this phenomenon took place because of the high number of practitioners who contributed only once". Our findings show that practitioners contributed significantly to the citation spikes in 2007 and 2010. These results build on the role of practitioners in science innovation. Several authors write about the academia–practice divide, also known as the European paradox, because Europe is known for having a strong science base but weak innovation performance on the basis of this. According to Hodgkinson *et al.* (2001, p. 41), the "research-base of the business and management studies field is failing to meet the needs of various parties who are (or ought to be) valid stakeholders in the knowledge production process". Additionally, in a speech at the Academy of Management conference (reported by Huff, 2000, p. 55) James

G. March stated that "fundamental knowledge becomes more useful to managers in changing worlds, in new ventures, and when faced with the unexpected".

The results of this study show that practitioners are not only consumers of science innovation but also have an important role as producers of innovation. Evolution of technology as well as innovation in society (such as internationalization and globalization) create new ways of doing business, pushing practitioners to the front line of scientific innovation in business models, leaving academics behind. Most of the influential practitioner pieces in our study are conceptual works, typically published as books or working papers and not in traditional academic outlets with limited access to practitioners and policymakers. These results call for a new approach to science production, a transformative redefinition, that sees a greater involvement of policymakers and practitioners not only to develop research needs but also to learn from them.

Critique 2. What business model, and for whom

Consistent with Wirtz *et al.* (2010), the findings of this study indicate that more emphasis should be placed on the managerial process of the business model. The role of leadership and the evolution of traditional managerial tools, such as 'business plans' is recognized as a topic that deserves further research (Prahalad and Hammond, 2002; Tikkanen *et al.*, 2005). These results lead to questioning of the educational implications of the business model. According to Tapscott *et al.* (2000, p. 186) "the revolution in the net-enabled business model is intersecting with a demographic revolution which is changing the culture of work". Our findings illustrate that besides the e-business movement, business models provide new ways and different forms of value creation to customers, in turn reshaping the rules of business. However, none of the publications analyzed here focus on the educational implications of this movement, and thereby open up new research opportunities.

The concept of the business model is largely applied to private or listed companies. But what about the public sector? Developing a search on Scopus for the words 'Business Model*' returns 18,408 articles. In adding the words 'public sector', Scopus returns only 142 articles.[1] As suggested by Kaplan (2011, p. 4)

business models aren't just for business ... if an organization has a viable way to create, deliver, and capture value, it has a business model. It doesn't matter whether an organization is in the public or private sector. It doesn't matter if it's a non-profit or a for-profit enterprise. All organizations have a business model.

However, even though business model research can be extended to different sectors (public versus private, profit versus non-profit) and organizational dimensions (big versus small), public sector business models deserve a separate research agenda. For example, as suggested by Massaro *et al.* (2015, p. 530) "the public sector is organizationally specific, has different effectiveness concerns and has different levels of representativeness, accountability, and responsiveness". Similarly, "SMEs are not smaller versions of large firms" (Olejnik, 2014), and medium size firms should receive more attention due to their importance in supporting national growth in many countries (Massaro *et al.*, 2016b, p. 278). Therefore, new research opportunities can be seen in extending the business model research agenda to the public sector and varying enterprise sizes such as SMEs.

Critique 3. Sustainable value and stakeholder involvement

According to Hart and Milstein (2003, p. 56), "the global challenges associated with sustainable development are also multifaceted, involving economic, social, and environmental concerns". While value and value creation is a well-investigated topic, only a few studies focus on different meanings of value. Few of the works present in our sample of influential business model contributions are positioned within sustainability and social innovation, where value is sought and dispersed more equally to the stakeholders that encompass the firm and its immediate partnerships (Tweedie *et al.*, forthcoming). This indicates that the economic logic underpinning the understanding of mainstream business models should be redefined. For example, Seelos and Mair (2005, p. 242) report the case of OneWorld Health, which

> has adopted an entrepreneurial business model to deliver medicines to those most in need in developing countries. It aims to redesign the whole value chain of drug delivery, and so challenges traditional profitability thinking, which seems incompatible with developing the much-needed cures.

Therefore, the business model literature should be open to different value concepts, extending to sustainability and corporate social responsibility, since they can create "novel business models, organizational structures, and strategies for brokering between very limited and disparate resources to create social value" (Seelos and Mair, 2005, p. 244). Similarly, research should be extended to emerging countries.

Transformative redefinitions

This section aims to answer the third research question: What are the likely future scenarios for business model research? The transformative redefinition addresses the need to reconceptualize what we learn from insights and critique; it "directs us to avoid hyper critique and negativity through taking the notion of critical pragmatism and positive action seriously" (Alvesson and Deetz (2000, p. 20). Subsequently, our analyses uncover that the field of business model research has reached a level of maturity and that there are four distinct stages of business model research that point towards future business model research opportunities and help us to pose a set of research questions for the academic community. This probing is necessary because, throughout the literature, business models are readily defined as a wonderful invention, a new unit of analysis for academics and practitioners and a concept that has the ability to develop businesses and hence create value and wealth for the generations to come. These are rhetorical diffusions that we must consider with caution.

Perhaps it is true that business models are a new conceptualization that really does make a difference to organizations. However, if we avoid work that is critical of the concept, has limitations and outlines the potential negative consequences of the business model for firms, we are guilty of limiting our investigations. Like innovation studies, business model research often outlines how different buisness models may create wealth when successful (Johnson *et al.*, 2008). None of the publications in our review analyzed business model failure.[2] A research agenda that only reveals the good news is incomplete and inadequate. We claim that future research should also address the limitations of the business model concept and the negative effects that it may cause for the development and management of companies and other types of organization.

In this context, it is useful to recall the work of Sveiby (2012, p. 1) who addresses the concepts of managerial incompetence and of unintended consequences when exploring the development of a radical financial innovation, that is, securitization. He mantains that

> This innovation changed the context for all actors in the financial industry repeatedly to such a degree that even the highest regarded experts repeatedly made prediction errors. The negative effects of prediction errors have since 1980 gradually became larger until today when even a single individual decision by a portfolio manager may risk global financial mayhem.

All in all, this underlines the need to to train managers to be adaptable to new scenarios rather than teaching them to deal with known conditions.

It is clear from the data presented here that the field of business model research has developed over time. New themes emerge and become more dominant, while others decline in interest; some even return to the spotlight in revitalized formats. The methodology applied in this study does not track the field of business models by the number of works published, but instead according to the work that is highly cited, and thereby dominant. It may therefore be the case that there are alternative themes that are emerging in the literature, but just not being cited very often – yet.

According to our analytical framework, we analyzed papers considering their evolution over time, in terms of number of papers and citations (the first level of 'when'). The second level is based on the 'who' dimensions, with the aim to analyze who are the most prominent authors in the discipline and to understand the role of practitioners: author demographics are recorded focusing on the number of publications by each author and the background of the first author. We also make a distinction between academics and non-academics. The third and fourth levels focus, respectively, on the 'what' and 'how' dimensions, addressing the research questions and methods used for reaching an understanding of the scientific maturity of the field. Lastly, the fifth level of analysis focuses on 'which', where we distinguish between practical and research implications.

We argue that there currently are four dominant stages of business model research present in the field, and identifying these four stages allows for identification of future scenarios.

Concerning the 'what', several thematic gaps revealed themselves in our four sub-conclusions to Chapters 5–8, and these gaps provide new, relevant contexts and opportunities for business model research.

We cannot deny that the lack of a well-defined theoretical foundation, a general accepted definition of the terms 'business model' and 'business model innovation' and a general classification scheme for business models (taxonomies) represent significant gaps for the business model research. And we call for further research on these, taking the knowledge created over the four stages as a point of departure.

Concerning business model design, in accordance with Zott and Amit (2013), future research should investigate how and why new business models are designed in companies, how the design process is planned and executed, which levers and barriers may arise during the process, who are the key actors, and which tools and managerial practices are used to achieve consistency among

- the designed business model;
- the company's strategy, processes, and activity system; and
- the value chain and the ecosystem where the company operates.

Once designed, a business model has to be implemented; we maintain that future research should test tools and managerial practices to help practitioners in executing this step. Here too, key actors have to be identified, and levers and barriers have to be explored so that the first can be capitalized and the latter can be limited. Moreover, in accordance with Arend (2013), it would be interesting to investigate how multiple business models can be implemented and managed simultaneously within the same company.

With regard to business model innovation, we argue that future research should aim at developing and enriching the current business model patterns library to enable business model innovation practices within companies, that is, challenging the status quo and triggering new business model development patterns. Currently, the most complete approaches are those of Gassmann *et al.* (2014) and Taran *et al.* (2016), who identify 55 and 71 business model patterns, respectively. Due to the hypercompetitive and dynamic environment, these lists are by no means final, but they will evolve over time: some new business model patterns will emerge and will become dominant, while others will decline and maybe disappear. Thus, the process of updating the list of available business model patterns is a never-ending one; keeping this list up to date is a very relevant task because it ensures that companies can innovate their business model by gaining inspiration from the latest value creation and value capture logics available in their or in other industries.

Additionally, we argue that it would be fruitful to conduct research to shed light on the dominant business model patterns in specific industries to understand if, and to what extent, companies are differentiated from each other. This would lead to the investigation of relevant research questions like the following: do companies compete on similar or different business models? Do companies properly use the business model innovation space available to them? Or is the competition very intense due to the use of a limited portfolio of business model patterns? Do business model imitation phenomena take place? Why and how does it happen?

In accordance with Schneider and Spieth (2013) and Spieth *et al.* (2014), we also maintain that the antecedents ('why') and the timing ('when') of business model innovation have to be explored, as well as the levers and the barriers that can enable or hinder this process.

Implementing or innovating a business model entails performance implications that are worthy of analysis. In particular, we assume that different business model patterns will impact on the performance in different ways (e.g. higher revenues, faster time to market, stronger customer lock in, higher channel effectiveness). Thus, it would be interesting to look more closely at the relationships between the adoption of certain business model patterns and organizational performance.

Finally, the measurement and the disclosure dimensions of the business model need to be explored. In particular, we argue that the business model is a fruitful level of abstraction to extract key performance indicators able to provide managers with information on the ability of a company to create and capture value. In other words, using the business model as a platform to extract key performance indicators has the potential to improve the relevance of a performance measurement system because it can direct the measurement process to focus only on the material aspects of value creation. Until now, there has been little discussion about how the business model perspective can support performance measurement (Montemari and Chiucchi, 2017; Nielsen and Roslender, 2015; Nielsen *et al.*, 2009), and some aspects require and deserve additional attention:

- the process that leads from business model to building measures;
- the levers and the barriers that can arise during this process; and
- the pros and the cons of using the business model for measurement purposes.

Beyond the interaction between business models and performance measurement, we also maintain that another relevant issue to be faced concerns how the business model is presented in corporate external disclosures. As there are no guidelines on how to disclose the business model, the effectiveness of this task often depends on the competences and the skills of the developers who actually design and implement disclosure tools in companies. For the sake of comparability of business model disclosures in time and space, we call for further research on how to present the business model in corporate external disclosures (e.g. the choice and the implementation of the technique to map the business model, how to identify the items to be measured and disclosed, and so on).

The 'what' dimension is somehow related to the context where the business model concept is analyzed. Our SLR has shown that the business model concept has been largely applied to private, for profit or listed companies. Therefore, new research opportunities can be found in extending the business model research agenda on the 'what' dimension to the public sector and the non-profit sector, and varying enterprise sizes such as SMEs. In this respect, we claim that exploring the relationships between business models and the notions of sustainability and more socially fair dispersions of value is an important avenue of research.

Also, our SLR has revealed that there are no relevant studies published in any emerging countries such as China, South America or African countries. We believe that these under-studied contexts will provide fruitful avenues of future research.

Regarding the 'when' dimension, it is of course difficult to predict precisely when research contributions in the future are novel enough to produce research spikes such as those evident in our current data, but we expect the field to continue to proceed through citation spikes from time to time. The current analysis reveals that spikes tend to be practitioner-driven; therefore, we might speculate as to what could possibly spur new types of practitioner interest. Economic and political movements such as changes in trade structures, global reforms, recessions or economic growth may cause interest because new models of doing business will become viable. However, our data suggests that spikes are more likely to be associated with technology shocks, increased digital disruption and Smart City developments in conjunction with Industry 4.0 and Internet of Things conjectures.

Concerning the 'who' dimension, we expect practitioners and academics to cooperate intensively to develop the next stages of business model research. On the one hand, we foresee practitioners playing a key role in the next citation spikes, as happened in 2007 and 2010, and following the trend started at the beginning of the millenium. Here we see practitioners not only as consumers of knowledge but also as relevant producers of knowledge on business models.

On the other hand, we argue that it is time for academics to get their hands dirty inside companies, through interventionist research to apply and test business model tools, to understand what really happens when a business model is designed, implemented, innovated, measured or disclosed. Reflecting on these experiences would provide insights on what does and does not work, as well as on the reasons behind successful and unsuccessful experiences, that is, business model success or failure. In turn, fostering the dialogue between academics and practitioners will ensure that important issues are faced and helps to avoid the creation of a theory–practice gap.

This consideration leads itself to address the 'how' dimension of our analytical framework. Regarding research method, the SLR has revealed a predominance of papers that are conceptual in nature, which is typical of emerging fields. For the future, we expect a more balanced picture, in which theoretical and empirical contributions will play a more relevant role to advance the literature. In particular, we foresee contributions aimed at shedding light on the theoretical underpinnings of the business model concept, so that cumulative empirical inquiries can be developed.

Following along these lines, our SLR has shown that only 38% of the analyzed papers present one or more research questions, but the percentage of papers stating research questions increases over time. We expect that this trend will continue in this direction, and that researchers will be able to draw on the work of others more and more effectively. This trend should go hand in hand with the development of a shared and common accepted language. All in all, the combination of these two factors is likely to enhance the transparency and scientific maturity of the business model research area.

Finally, the analysis of the 'which' dimension has highlighted that only a few publications specifically report practical implications, mainly related to the need for understanding the components of the business model and to business model innovation. Managerial implications revolve around the consideration that managers have now to deal with a turbulent and dynamic competitive environment. We foresee an increasing attention on practical and managerial implications for the future, overall related to the (positive or negative) effects that the business model concept and tools cause within companies. Moreover, we expect growing attention on implications for policymakers and educational implications, which currently have been given little attention in under-researched contexts, such as public sector organizations and emerging markets.

In contrast to the current situation highlighted by our SLR, we also imagine increasing attention on research implications, mainly related to the avenues of research that we have identified when we discussed the 'what' dimension of our analytical framework.

The following chapters of this manuscript analyze the existing knowledge base in business model research by identifying four distinct stages. In particular, Chapter 5 analyzes the first stage of business model research by focusing on definitions and conceptualizations of business models as well as on the links between business models and strategy; Chapter 6 frames the content of the second stage, dominated by the research stream of business model innovation; the design of frameworks and the foundations for theory-building are at the core of Chapter 7, which addresses the third stage of business model research; Chapter 8 investigates the fourth stage of business model research, centred on the relationship between business models and performance.

Notes

1 Search performed 18 August 2016.
2 Tretheway (2004) is an example of a relevant case study that analyzes the failure of network airline business models from the pressure of the no-frills business models of the low-cost competitors (Taran *et al.*, 2016).

5 First stage business model research

Definitions and concepts

Dominant authors in the first stage of business model research are typically already highly cited authors in related fields such as innovation (Henry Chesbrough), strategy (Michael Porter) and management (David Teece) and so might have a greater chance of being cited. They typically focus on the relations between the business model and their own fields of interest and use this to define the concept through similarities and differences. A good example of this is Magretta's (2002) account of the relationship between business models and strategy. The dominant authors in this first stage do not share ideas, but their game plans are identical. Practitioner insights also play a significant role in developing and forming the field through typological frameworks and definitions. Timmers (1998) and Petrovic *et al.* (2001) provide good examples of this. Following Critique 1 in Chapter 4, policymakers and practitioners need to be engaged to ensure that they are part of co-developing and learning from these insights.

Because the contributions of this stage of research were fragmented, there was a distinct lack of research concerning the different functions of business models, that is, as sensemaking tools (Michea, 2016), as tools for optimizing businesses and profits, controlling the actions of employees or fostering creativity and innovation. Taking these points into consideration leads to the presentation of two existing research paths discussed later, namely research into existing business model definitions and the relationship between business models and strategy.

Existing 'business model' definitions

There is no generally accepted definition of business model (Jensen, 2014). For this reason, the need to delimit the nature and components of a model and determine what constitutes a good model is a challenging task. There is also some confusion around terminology, as business model, strategy, business concept, revenue model and economic model are often used interchangeably (Seddon *et al.*, 2004). Moreover, the business model has also been referred to as architecture, design, pattern, plan, method, assumption and statement. At the most rudimentary level, the business model is defined solely in terms of the firm's economic model.

This section comprises a review of existing business model definitions and the respective background perspectives from which they emerge. There is consensus as to the fact that no unambiguous definition exists (Chesbrough and Rosenbloom, 2002; Hedman and Kalling, 2003; Porter, 2001) and that the theoretical grounding of most business model definitions is fragile (Groth and Nielsen, 2015). The analysis finds four overall background perspectives on which business model definitions can be allocated, based on their characteristics: systems of representation, resource-based views of firm performance, external prerequisites for profitability and internal prerequisites for profitability. In relation to the latter, Itami and Nishino (2010) argue that a business model is composed of two elements, a business system and a profit model, hence the term business model.

There are multiple perspectives of the purpose of working with business models, for example, relating to their role, and the perceived advantages of departing from a business model perspective. Osterwalder (2001, p. 2), for example, offers the following definition of an objective:

> Business models have two essential functions. First, they allow managers to talk about possible implementations of strategic objectives and understand the relevant issues. Secondly, an appropriately formulated business model can help managers easily express what they expect from people on the business process level or from technically oriented people.

There are clear linkages to creating an understanding of the overall functioning of the firm in Osterwalder's definition and a focus on communicating management's perceptions of the business to its staff. Highlighting these thoughts on creating a common understanding of the business, its strategy and objectives within the entire enterprise, Hoerl (1999) argues that applying a business model helps to structure the addressing of key business issues and, furthermore, that an effective business model ought to incorporate aspects such as culture, values and governance. One possible definition of a business model is offered by Nielsen (2010, p. 4):

A business model describes the coherence in the strategic choices that facilitate the handling of the processes and relations, which create value on both the operational, tactical and strategic levels in the organization. The business model is therefore the platform, which connects resources, processes and the supply of a service, which results in the fact that the company is profitable in the long term.

This specific definition emphasizes the need to focus on understanding the connections and the interrelations of the business and its operations so that the core of a business model description is the connections that create value. But the definition also reveals the theoretical perspective by using the term "operational, tactical and strategic levels in the organization", which points to elements of management control.

Nielsen (2010) argues that by contemplating the silos by which companies are normally managed, we become bogged down in endless descriptions of customer relations, employee competences, knowledge sharing, innovation activities and corporate risks that do not tell the business model story. However, if we start asking how these different elements interrelate, which changes among them need to be monitored and what the status is on operations, strategy and the activities initiated to create a unique value proposition, we will start to get a feel for how the chosen business model is performing. In this manner, most business model definitions can be scrutinized and analyzed, revealing the many differing theoretical perspectives represented in this literature.

When we survey the business model literature overall, we can easily identify more than 60 business model definitions. Table 4 outlines a selection of business model definitions to give an impression of their similarities and differences.

The survey in the later sections attempts to structure the existing business model definitions. These sections are structured so that first, we consider the generic types of business model definitions, that is, definitions concentrating solely on which elements such models ought to be comprised of for them to qualify as business models. This will give us an indication of the elements considered necessary for creating value from a business perspective, and also how we can differentiate business models from other related concepts and areas of research such as supply chain management (see, for example, Mason and Leek, 2008) and organizations in general. There is no doubt, however, that there exists a great deal of overlap between business models and other concepts within business research, such as the value chain and strategy.

Table 4 Selected business model definitions

Author	Definition	Comments
Slywotsky (1996)	"Business models refer to the totality of how a company selects its customers, defines and differentiates its offerings, defines the tasks it will perform itself and those it will outsource, configures its resources, goes to market, creates utility for customers and captures profits."	The business model is conceptualized as a mix of decisions to generate profits.
Timmers (1998)	"Business model stands for the architecture for the product, service and information flows, including a description of the various business actors and their roles, the potential benefits for these actors and the sources of revenues, the business model includes competition and stakeholders".	A broad definition that includes the internal and external actors, their roles, the tangible and intangible flows among them, and the source of revenues.
Venkatraman and Henderson (1998)	"An architecture along three dimensions: customer interaction, asset configuration and knowledge leverage".	A generic and concise definition, focused solely on which elements a business model should include.
Selz (1999)	"A business model is architecture for the firm's product, service and information flows. This includes a description of the various economic agents and their roles. A business model also describes the potential benefits for the various agents and provides a description of the potential revenue flows".	A broad definition, very consistent with that of Timmers (1998).
Mayo and Brown (1999)	"Business models refer to the design of key interdependent systems that create and sustain a competitive business."	The focus of this definition is on the aim of a business model: creating and sustaining a competitive business. The components of a business model are not identified.
Stewart and Zhao (2000)	"Business model is a statement of how a firm will make money and sustain its profit stream over time".	The financial sustainability over time is at the core of this definition.

(Continued)

Author	Definition	Comments
Linder and Cantrell (2000)	"The business model is the organization's core logic for creating value".	A very concise definition, focused solely on the internal dimension of creating value.
Hamel (2000)	"A business model is simply a business concept that has been put into practice. A business concept has four major components: Core Strategy, Strategic Resources, Customer Interface and Value Network … (Elements of the core strategy include business mission, product/market scope, and basis for differentiation. Strategic resources include core competencies, key assets, and core processes. Customer interface includes fulfillment and support, information and insight, relationships and pricing structure. The value network consists of suppliers, partners and coalitions)".	A very detailed definition focused on business model components. Interestingly enough, the core strategy is considered a dimension of the business model.
Porter (2001)	"The definition of a business model is murky at best. Most often, it seems to refer to a loose conception of how a company does business and generates revenue. Yet simply having a business model is an exceedingly low bar set for building a company. […] The business model approach to management becomes an invitation for faulty thinking and self-delusion".	A very critical definition, highlighting the ambiguity of the concept.
Petrovic *et al.* (2001)	"Business model describes the logic of a business system for creating value that lies behind the actual processes".	Similar to Linder and Cantrell (2000), this definition focuses on the internal dimension of creating value.
Weill and Vitale (2001)	"A description of the roles and relationships among a firm's consumers, customers, allies and suppliers that identifies major flows of product, information and money and the major benefits to participants".	Similar to Timmers (1998), a broad definition focused on actors involved and on the tangible and intangible flows among them.

Magretta (2002)	"Business models are stories that explain how the enterprises work" With the enhanced explanation: "Business models describe, as a system, how the pieces of a business fit together, but they don't factor in one critical dimension of performance: competition" … "a good business model has to satisfy two conditions. It must have a good logic – who the customers are, what they value, and how the company can make money by providing them that value. Second, the business model must generate profits."	The conditions of a successful business model are at the core of this definition. Interestingly enough, the focus in on the relationships among components. The strategic dimension (competition) is kept apart from the business model concept.
Osterwalder (2004)	"A conceptual tool that contains a set of elements and their relationships and allows expressing the business logic of a specific firm. It is a description of the value a company offers to one or several segments of customers and the architecture of the firm and its network of partners for creating, marketing and delivering this value and relationship capital, to generate profitable and sustainable revenue stream".	This definition is centred on the components of a business model and on the relationships among them.
Chesbrough (2006)	"The business model is a useful framework to link ideas and technologies to economic outcomes" … "It also has value in understanding how companies of all sizes can convert technological potential (e.g. products, feasibility, and performance) into economic value (price and profits)" … "Every company has a business model, whether that model is articulated or not".	The business model is viewed as an enabler to convert technologies into economic outcomes.
Skarzynski and Gibson (2008)	"The business model is a conceptual framework for identifying how a company creates, delivers, and extracts value. It typically includes a whole set of integrated components, all of which can be looked on as opportunities for innovation and competitive advantage".	The business model is seen as a source of competitive advantage and innovation. The focus is on value creation, delivery and capture.
Zott and Amit (2008)	"The business model is a structural template of how a focal firm transacts with customers, partners, and vendors; that is, how it chooses to connect with factor and product markets. It refers to the overall gestalt of these possibly interlinked boundary-spanning transactions."	This definition focuses on the whole enterprise system and how the firm is positioned in the overall value chain.

Next, the review takes a closer look at business models understood as the whole enterprise system and how the firm is positioned in the value chain – or whether their focus is on the specific causal links between organizational activities, processes and the like, and do not consider external aspects.

Within each category, there are a number of subcategories to which the business model definitions may relate. The subcategories are somewhat more specific, for example, whether the definitions incorporate aspects of representativeness, strategy, value proposition or value creation. The review, discussion and analysis of the characteristics of the definitions in each of these gives interesting insight into which generic elements are thought of as comprising a business model and which building blocks are thought to be the most important elements (see, for example, Johnson *et al.*, 2008). Finally, this overview looks at different opinions relating to incorporating both broad and narrow components into a business model. The objective of the review here is to get closer to what a good business model definition must encompass.

Some business model definitions and conceptualizations encompass not only the company itself, but the entire value creation system of which it is a part – typically the value chain, that is, including business relationships such as suppliers and customers and taking external forces into account (see, for example, Anderson *et al.*, 2009). This group of definitions is characterized by a focus on describing the method of doing business by which the company seeks to sustain itself, including both internal and external aspects. Sustainability is often equated to making money and value creation (see also Yip, 2004). Incorporating business relationships into these definitions distinguishes them from narrow definitions, for example, by including the value proposition of the firm (Wirtz *et al.*, 2010). We now look at the existing business model definitions that can be characterized as broad.

According to Timmers (1998), a business model is the architecture for product, service and information flows, including a description of the various business actors and their roles; a description of the potential benefits for the various business actors; and a description of the sources of revenues. Timmers' definition is extremely broad and to some degree also rather unspecific. It could probably be categorized as a generic definition. However, as it includes elements of representation (see also Schafer *et al.*, 2005) and value proposition, it relates more to specific definitions. A similar definition, in that it too has a focus on representation and value proposition, is that of Weill and Vitale (2001). They define a business model as "a description of the roles and relationships among a firm's consumers, customers, allies and suppliers that identifies the major flows of product, information, and money, and the major benefits to participants". This too is a very broad definition, in essence covering all possible aspects of doing business.

A number of the definitions within this category have explicit connections with the term sustainability. Sustainability is, in essence, the company's ability to create revenue in the long term. Thus, there is a weak linkage to the generic definitions that focused on profits and revenue. According to Afuah and Tucci (2000, p. 2), a business model describes "how [the firm] plans to make money long-term", and they define such a model as one incorporating the following components: customer value, scope, pricing, revenue source, connected activities, implementation, capabilities and sustainability (through the firm's unique value configuration). KPMG offers the following definition: "The fundamental logic by which the enterprise creates sustained economic value – the organization's 'business model'" (2001, p. 3, 11). The terms 'fundamental logic' and 'value configuration' resemble Stabell and Fjeldstad's value configuration logics (1998), and again these definitions cover all possible aspects of doing business.

Similarly, Rappa's definition (2001) states that "a business model is the method of doing business by which a company can sustain itself – that is, generate revenue. The business model spells out how a company makes money by specifying where it is positioned in the value chain". In addition to departing from the notion of sustainability, it also incorporates a more specific notion of the position of the firm in the value chain.

Chesbrough and Rosenbloom (2002, p. 5) offer

> the business model as a construct that integrates these earlier perspectives into a coherent framework that takes technological characteristics and potentials as inputs, and converts them through customers and markets into economic outputs. The business model is thus conceived as a focusing device that mediates between technology development and economic value creation. We argue that firms need to understand the cognitive role of the business model, to commercialize technology in ways that will allow firms to capture value from their technology investments.

In continuation of this, Chesbrough and Rosenbloom identify a number of attributes of a business model which ultimately should enable the company to articulate its value proposition, identify a market segment, define the structure of the value chain within which it operates, estimate profit potentials and formulate a competitive strategy. A similarly comprehensive definition is Marrs and Mundt's (2001, p. 28):

> A business model is designed to compile, integrate, and convey information about an organization's business and industry. Ideally, it depicts the entire system, both internal and external, within which the organization operates. Not only does the construction of a model help management better understand the structure, nature, and direction of their organization, but it provides a basis for communicating such information to employees and other interested stakeholders. The model can be the catalyst for developing a shared understanding of what the entity is today and what needs to be done to move to some desired future state.

Regarding the applied detail of the business model, Marrs and Mundt state that it should be "as detailed as users deem necessary to fit their needs, also availability of information is a constrainer" (2001, p. 28).

The application of a business model can facilitate the following: gaining an understanding of the whole business; facilitating a common understanding of the business by others; identifying opportunities for process improvements; identifying and mitigating business risks; developing the basis for (process) performance measurement; and facilitating the development of the enterprise's directional course. Overall, they state that there are two applications of business models: first, communicating the nature of the business, and second, improving the business (e.g. strategic analysis, business process analysis, business performance measurement, risk assessment). Marrs and Mundt's definition relates to the entire business system and especially facilitating understanding, with the outcome being an improvement of the business. Likewise, Doz and Kosonen (2010) incorporate relationships between a firm and its customers.

According to Bell *et al.*,

> the (client) business model is a strategic-systems decision frame that describes the interlinking activities carried out within a business entity, the external forces that bear upon the entity, and the business relationships with persons and other organizations outside of the entity.
>
> (1997, pp. 37–39)

Six components of a business model are identified in the 'Strategic-Systems Auditing' framework: External forces, markets formats, business processes (strategic management process, core business processes, resource management processes), alliances, core products and services and customers. This definition is value chain influenced by, and at the same focused on, internal processes and value drivers. There is clearly a change in focus between the 1997 and the 2002 definitions of the 'Strategic-Systems Auditing' framework, as will be evident in the next section, the latter being more narrowly defined with a value driver focus.

Magretta (2002, p. 4) perceives business models as "stories that explain how enterprises work", explaining that a business model not only shows how the firm makes money but also by answering the fundamental questions: Who is the customer? And what does the customer value? In this sense, she touches upon performativity, as is also evident in Perkmann and Spicer (2010). Finally, Morris (2003) argues that a business model defines a broad competitive approach to business and articulates how a company applies processes (Mansfield and Fourie, 2004) and technologies to build and sustain effective relationships with customers. These relationships are the most critical factor. Creating them, understanding them, preserving them, enriching them and extending them are the critical attributes of success. Everything that is done must be in service to these relationships; they are the point. In summary, some of these definitions can be rather difficult to distinguish from generic definitions. One rule of thumb, however, is that they are closer to a 'how' objective than merely describing a 'what' objective. Also, they treat the business model as a system of representation and consider the long-term performance of the firm, whereas the generic definition is more apt to focus on resources necessary for value creation (see, for example, Verstraete and Jouison-Laffitte, 2011).

Other business model definitions include only intra-firm components, that is, infrastructure, processes, value drivers, all prerequisites for value creation. As opposed to the broad definitions, they do not incorporate relationships external to the entity, that is, customers, suppliers or other external forces.

Along these lines, Petrovic *et al.* (2001) argue that a business model is not a description of a complex social system itself with all its actors, relations and processes, as opposed to what is stated in the broad definitions. Instead, they contend, "it describes the logic of a 'business system' for creating value that lies behind the actual processes. A business model is the conceptual and architectural implementation of a business strategy and the foundation for the implementation of business processes and Information Systems". Concentrating solely on the internal aspects pertaining to value creation, this definition naturally must be classified as a narrow definition. This definition includes elements of strategy (see also Smith *et al.*, 2010) and representation and the authors argue that a business model ought not to be too broad and should concentrate on specific elements pertaining to value creation.

Similarly, Boulton *et al.* (2000) emphasize the need to create a business model that links combinations of assets to value creation (see also Björkdahl, 2009 for a similar perspective). Having defined the business model in their earlier book *Cracking the Value Code* as "[t]he unique combination of tangible and intangible assets that drives an organization's ability to create or destroy value" (Boulton *et al.*, 1997, p. 244), these definitions relate to the business model as a detailed account for the internal prerequisites for value creation, as there is a clear value driver and value creation focus. The mention of "assets" also hints to a resource-based view in the early version. Bell and Solomon (2002, p. xi) define the business model as "a simplified representation of the network of causes and effects that determine the extent to which the entity creates value and earns profits". This definition is based on a somewhat simplified version of the definition and ideas from the KPMG Business Measurement Process research published in Bell *et al.* (1997). It is a narrow, definition and it has a predominantly internal focus, as opposed to the 1997 definition, which incorporates the elements of value drivers, value creation and representation.

Even more focused on value drivers and processes is Bray's (2002, p. 13) definition: "The business model is defined by the performance drivers, business processes, people and the infrastructure put in place to achieve the company's business objectives". Bray's explicit link to business objectives is also a link to strategy and – especially – value creation, although this is not specifically stated. Value creation is, however, somewhat more explicitly mentioned in Linder and Cantrell's (2002, p. 1) business model definition: "A real business model is the organization's core logic for creating value". More specifically, it is the following (Linder and Cantrell, 2002, p. 5):

- The set of value propositions an organization offers to its stakeholders,
- Along with the operating processes to deliver on these,
- Arranged as a coherent system,
- That both relies on and builds assets, capabilities and relationships to create value.

They elaborate further by clarifying that a business model should explain how the organization offers unique value and be difficult to imitate, grounded in reality and able to help in ensuring that different stakeholders are speaking the same language. Here is a clear link between business models and performance, which is likewise found in Doganova and Eyquem-Renault (2009).

Like Magretta's ideas on strategy and the business model, Sandberg (2002) acknowledges that although strategy is not an inherent part of the business model, there is a very close connection between the two. Quoting Porter (1996), Sandberg states that competitive strategy is about being different and that the business model is the vehicle for operationalizing these differences. A well-constructed business model focuses employees on the activities that really add value (i.e. via facilitating understanding). To fulfil this purpose, a business model should follow the following steps:

1   Identify the customers you want to serve;
2   Spell out how your business is different from all the others – its unique value proposition;
3   Explain how you will implement the value proposition; and
4   Describe the profit patterns, the associated cash flows, and the attendant risks (see also Mullins and Komisar, 2009, for a more recent discussion of this perspective).

Business models and strategy

Moving to the relationship between business models and strategy (see also Ammar, 2006; Seddon *et al.*, 2004; Yip, 2004), Zott and Amit (2008) analyze the fit between product market strategy and business models. Their findings suggest that novelty-centred business models, that is, differentiation-based business models and not business models based on efficiency – coupled with product market strategies that emphasize differentiation, cost leadership or early market entry – can enhance firm performance. In a later study, Amit and Zott (2012) argue that competitive advantage (through business models) can be achieved through the mechanisms of creating novelty, lock-in, complementarity or efficiency and that business model innovation can occur in a number of ways – but typically in three categories:

1   by adding novel activities, for example, through forward or backward integration – we refer to this form of business model innovation as new activity system 'content';
2   by linking activities in novel ways – we refer to this form of business model innovation as new activity system 'structure'; and

3   by changing one or more parties that perform any of the activities –
we refer to this form of business model innovation as new activity
system 'governance'.

As is evident, the connections among value creation, business models
and strategy are close. Sweet (2001) acknowledges this connection and
argues that the management of fundamental strategic value configuration logics, such as relationships to suppliers, access to technologies,
insight into users' needs, and so on, is far more relevant than inventing
new revolutionary business models, an opinion supported by Ramirez
(1999) and Stabell and Fjeldstad (1998). These arguments should, however, be put in perspective by remembering that Sweet (2001), in talk-
ing of new revolutionary business models, is thinking about e-business
models.

It is interesting to note that Chesbrough and Rosenbloom (2002)
take in strategy as an element of the business model, which suggests that the relationship between business models and strategy,
while perhaps not fuzzy, is yet to be decided. In her 2002 book,
Joan Magretta defines business models as "stories that explain how
enterprises work", and here she notes that strategy, understood as
how to outmanoeuvre your competitors, is something different from
a business model. However, we must remember that Joan Magretta
is Michael Porter's colleague, and as such, she may be influenced
by the competitive-based school of strategy. Later, Seddon *et al.*
(2004) take part in this discussion by schematizing the possibilities
in Figure 13.

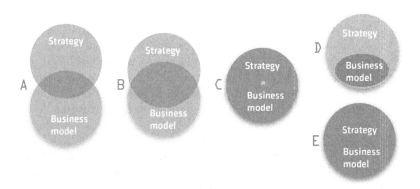

Figure 13 Possible concept overlaps between business models and strategy
(adapted from Seddon *et al.*, 2004).

We can use this logic to discuss different authors' takes on the relationship between business models and strategy. For example, we recap Nielsen's (2010, p. 4) business model definition given earlier:

> A business model describes the coherence in the strategic choices which facilitates the handling of the processes and relations which create value on both the operational, tactical and strategic levels in the organization. The business model is therefore the platform which connects resources, processes and the supply of a service which results in the fact that the company is profitable in the long term.

Thus, it is evident that it takes the stance of Seddon *et al.*'s (2004) option E because it sees the business model as the platform that enables strategy execution (see Brousseau and Penard, 2007, for a discussion of the economics of platforms). Further discussion in this realm might go into further detail about the level of organization at which this discussion is taking place. It might, for example, be pondered that a large multinational (conglomerate) has a strategy of pursuing many business models, while on the level of the Strategic Business Unit (SBU), it is the business that decides the action. Nielsen's business model definition might best be allocated to this SBU-level contribution.

Transformative redefinition: relevant first stage business model research paths

- There is no general accepted definition of business model. The need to delimit the nature and components of a model and determine what constitutes a good model is the task of the first stage.
- Business model researchers need to be critical of the business model concept and its defining elements. Future research should address the limitations of the concept and the potential negative consequences it may have for the development and management of firms and other types of organizations. Among the problems with the concept of business models is that there is obvious disagreement among terminologies related to business models. For example, 'strategy', 'business concept', 'revenue model' and 'economic model' are used as interchangeable terms. In addition, a business model is compared to architecture, a design, a pattern, a plan, a method, an assumption and even a statement, and thus there is also disagreement about the form a business model should take.

Our study here shows a distinct lack of highly cited research concerning the different functions that business models could have in a firm setting, for example, as mechanisms of control, development or sense-making. Perhaps the concept of business models might even take several or all of these functions in the firm at the same time, but through different levels of abstraction and through different organizational and managerial processes. Research should critically try to establish relationships between the functions of business models, applied levels of abstraction and the level of organization at which they are applied. Finally, this may be related to the pre-existing processes by which business models are transported throughout the firm.

6 Second stage business model research

The innovation of business models

Dominant authors in the second stage of business model research had similar characteristics to those of the first stage insofar as well-established authors in related fields were citation leaders. However, the theme of the research was altered to focus more on the innovation of business models and, to some extent, performance. The most highly cited publication is the practitioner piece by O'Reilly (2007), which conceptualizes several business model innovation patterns.[1] In this second stage of business model research, we see the beginnings of sounder theoretical work gaining momentum, best exemplified by Teece's (2007) dynamic capabilities article. Moreover, several contributions set about organizing the discussion. One of these contributions is that of Pateli and Giaglis (2004), who propose an analytic framework to decompose the area of business model research into eight research subdomains: definitions, components, conceptual models, design methods and tools, taxonomies, change methodologies, evaluation models and adoption factors.

While there were developments towards research questions concerning the dispersion of value between stakeholders surrounding a business model in the form of sustainability concerns in first-stage research, we find it surprising that the notions of business models from an ecosystem and value-sharing perspective are seemingly under-researched in the context of innovating business models in these directions. Some early work on social business models is present in our sample, but it mostly ignores, for example, ethics. The notion that this business model innovation stage is a mature area of research is confirmed by a recent study by Wirtz et al. (2016a), who argue that future research into this topic should aim at consolidating and confirming existing frameworks empirically.

Working with the understanding of the novelty of innovating cost/revenue structures, Kind et al. (2009) analyze how competitive forces may influence the way media firms like TV channels construct their revenue models. A media firm can either be financed by advertising revenue, by direct payment from the viewers (or the readers, if we consider newspapers) or by both. Kind *et al.* (2009) show that the competitiveness of the industry and the ease of substitution to alternative providers constrains the attractiveness of the advertisement-based revenue model. Bonaccorsi *et al.* (2006) also discuss the role of competition-levels in a setting of market-entry strategies in the software industry.

Another stream of literature where business thinking has played a major role in new modes of business is within social innovation, for example, by tapping into bottom of the pyramid (BoP) markets (Chesbrough, 2006). Seelos and Mair (2007) study the potential of creating profitable business models in a deep-poverty setting. Under the BoP approach, poor people are identified as potential customers who can be served profitably through value configurations that take their specific context and characteristics into account. However, companies that are used to competing in industrialized markets might need to fundamentally rethink their existing strategies and business models, which would involve acquiring and building new resources and capabilities and forging a multitude of local partnerships.

Despite an unusual setting, the studies on social innovation provide extreme situations and sound learning points that we can apply to the more generic forms of business model innovation. For example, from precisely such a BoP business model approach, Yunus *et al.* (2010) present a series of lessons learned in relation to achieving successful business model innovation from a longitudinal case study. They find that using business model thinking helps to challenge conventional thinking, find complementary partners and undertake continuous experimentation.

Innovation and technology

While strategy and management in relation to firms are concerned with how tactical and strategic moves are executed by managers to change or implement adjustments to the focal firm's business model, from the perspective of technology and innovation the contribution of business models adds a significant and dynamic dimension because it enables adjustments of exploitation. Johnson (2010) provides interesting insight into seizing new opportunities through business model innovation (see also Budde *et al.* 2012).

In his work with open innovation and open business model innovation, Henry Chesbrough (2006, 2007b) makes us consider the broader concept of 'open business models' in which the focal firm becomes a much more permeable economic space and boundary in terms of sharing product development, distribution and even other administrative functions with strategic partners. For example, large pharmaceutical companies might outsource product development to smaller biotechnology companies (see Brink and Holmen, 2009) while licensing technologies and access to markets modifies the business model (Casper, 2000). Thus, the operating architecture of the business model becomes a locus for innovation and recalibration.

The combination of leveraged cost and time savings with new revenue opportunities confers powerful advantages for companies willing to open their business models (Chesbrough, 2007b, p. 24). While Sosna *et al.* (2010) consider the antecedents and positive drivers of business model innovation in a Spanish dietary products business threatened by economic recession and heightened competition resulting from liberalization. In a later paper, Chesbrough (2010) considers the barriers to business model innovation in terms of inertia and a lack of entrepreneurial and managerial leadership that are required to experiment and effectuate change to a business model (Tikkanen *et al.*, 2005).

Andersson *et al.* (2011) construct a descriptive 'financialized biopharma business model' using three organizing elements: narratives about performance, capital market conditions and the variable motivation of equity investors (Andersson *et al.*, 2011, p. 631). This alternative framing of the biopharma business model reveals the complexity and risk attached to the business model (see also Bigliardi *et al.*, 2005) because all elements that help structure the descriptive model need to be aligned to reduce financial risk to investors (Sabatier *et al.*, 2012).

In a biotechnology–pharmaceutical setting, Haslam *et al.* (2010) construct a business model that reveals how the product innovation and development process conjoins with speculative forces in capital markets. Three organizing elements are employed for conceptualizing this descriptive business model: (1) narratives about pipeline progress that may (or may not) lead to additional funding from equity investors or other investing partners; (2) capital market conditions that impact on the supply of funding and market valuations; and (3) the variable motivations of equity investors who are not in a development marathon but a relay race where they are anxiously attempting to pass on ownership and extract higher returns on invested capital through realized market value. Hence, in this rather special biotechnology-pharmaceutical setting, where the companies are to be understood as constituted by investment portfolios of innovations and where products in the pipeline can be evaluated as risky future cash flows, capital providers trade for shareholder value according to their portfolio and trading strategies. In this speculative setting, capital market liquidity becomes a prominent variable and the customer needs – represented in the customer-centric school of thought in business models (see Richardson, 2008) – has minor or no influence at all.

Positing a slightly different view in a study on technology's effect on firm performance, De Carolis (2003, p. 44) finds that in the short term, building on prior stocks of knowledge and existing technology may be a superior strategy. In the long run, however, the development of new competences and application of new technologies will be crucial to future competitive advantage and survival. Therefore, innovation, with regard to technology and business model concepts is still an indispensable aspect of the business model discussion. For example, competition in the logistics industry has been changed drastically in recent years through the introduction and utilization of IT. Illustrating how these changes have led to closer collaboration between companies and their logistics partners, Velocci (2001) argues that the differences are so substantial that it gives meaning to talk of a whole new business model. Dell is an outstanding example of how a company has refined and extended an existing business model with IT. With the unique value proposition of its direct sales and built-to-order business model (Kraemer *et al.*, 1999), Dell has managed to influence how a whole industry does business.

E-business innovation

Internet technology has given rise to opportunities for top management to create new business models or to rediscover old ones. For instance, as noted by Rappa (2001), the Internet has allowed for the rediscovery of auctions. E-business in general has made it possible to enable transactions between companies in new and more frictionless manners – in this way creating value (Amit and Zott, 2001), because the Internet has connected businesses to other businesses or to consumers through either new value streams, revenue streams or logistical streams (Mahadevan, 2000).

A large proportion of the early work on business models was concerned with understanding the vast opportunities of Internet-based businesses (Mahadevan, 2000; Timmers, 1998). In 1998, Timmers had already classified ten generic types of Internet business models:

- e-shop;
- e-procurement;
- e-auction;
- third party marketplace;
- e-mall;
- virtual community;
- value chain integrator;
- information broker;
- value chain service provider; and
- collaboration platform.

Bambury (1998) described the business models that take place on the Internet by using two categories: transplanted real-world business models and native internet business models. The transplanted real-world business models include

- the mail-order model;
- the advertising-based model;
- the subscription model;
- the free trial model;
- the direct marketing model;
- the real estate model;
- the incentive scheme model;
- the business to business model; and
- combinations of these models.

The native Internet business models include (Bambury, 1998) the following:

- The library model. Internet represents a source of free information. Librarians, academics and scientists were among the first professional groups to grasp the potential of the public network for disseminating and making available free information.
- The freeware model. It is used by the Internet software community. Several software solutions, including popular Web browsers, are open sources and available for free download.
- The information barter model. It involves the exchange of information over the Internet between individuals and organizations. Sometimes, personal information may be sold to others to create

mailing lists or the information may be used to create profiles or customized advertising without the individual's consent.

• The digital products and the digital delivery model. Those products refer to images, movies, animation, audio, text, certificates and software. Digital delivery may take place when products are purchased or where information is bartered.

• The access provision model. This business provides access to the Internet with firms named Internet Service Providers (ISPs).

• Website hosting and other Internet services. Many ISPs provide services such as hosting Web servers, electronic mail, and URL and e-mail redirection services. Some firms provide free Web hosting and e-mail. These are usually financed by the inclusion of advertisements on certain sites and within e-mail.

Two years later, Rappa (2001) identified 41 types of Internet business models and classified them into nine categories, which were fairly similar to Weill and Vitale's eight (e-)business models from 2001, listed as follows:

1 *Content Providers.* Firms that provide information, products or services in a digital form to customers through third parties.

2 *Direct to Consumer.* Firms where the buyer and seller interact often bypassing traditional channel members.

3 *Full Service Providers.* Firms that provide a full service to totally match customer needs in a particular domain, consolidated through a single point of contact. Domains cover any area where customer needs cover multiple offerings.

4 *Intermediaries.* Firms that aim to link multiple buyers and sellers. Sellers pay the intermediary listing fees and selling commissions and it is possible that the buyer may pay a purchase or membership fee. Intermediaries are mostly electronic mall, shopping agents, electronic auctions and markets, specialty auctions and portals.

5 *Shared Infrastructure.* Firms that provide infrastructure shared by their owners offering a service that is not already available in the marketplace.

6 *Value Net Integrators.* Firms that coordinate product flows from suppliers to allies and customers. It strives to own the customer relationship with the other participants in the model and coordinates the value chain.

7 *Virtual Communities.* Firms in the centre of the model, situated between members of the community and suppliers. Members are able to communicate directly with each other.

8   *Whole-of-Enterprise/Government.* The single point of contact for
    the e-business customer is the essence of the whole-of-enterprise
    atomic business model. This model plays a relevant role in public
    sector organizations but also applies to the private sector.

One of the specific business model taxonomies created with the advent of e-business was the digital platform, and the recent literature
(Frankenberger *et al.*, 2013; Gassmann *et al.*, 2014) illustrates a number
of business model patterns based on platform thinking. Brousseau and
Penard (2007) analyze the economics of matching, the economics of
assembling and the economics of knowledge management in relation
to platform thinking and attempt to identify the principal trade-offs
at the core of choices among alternative digital business models and
compare them in terms of competitiveness and efficiency.

Conceptualizing the business model is therefore concerned with
identifying this platform, while analyzing it is concerned with gaining
an understanding of precisely which levers of control are appropriate
to deliver the value proposition of the company. Finally, communicating the business model is concerned with identifying the most important performance measures, both absolute and relative measures, and
relating them to the overall value creation story.

As argued earlier, a business model is neither just a value chain, nor
is it a corporate strategy. There exist many value configurations that
are different from that of a value chain, for example, value networks
and hubs. Rather, a business model is concerned with the unique combination of attributes that deliver a certain value proposition. Therefore, a business model is the platform that enables strategic choices to
become profitable. In some instances, it can be difficult to distinguish
between businesses that succeed because they are the best at executing a generic strategy and businesses that succeed because they have
unique business models. This is an important distinction to make, and
while some cases are clear-cut, others remain fuzzy.

Why is business model innovation crucial?

One of the best examples of a business model that has changed an existing industry is Ryanair, which has essentially restructured the business model of the airline industry (see also Casadesus-Masanell and
Ricart, 2011). As the air transport markets have matured, incumbent
companies that have developed sophisticated and complex business
models now face tremendous pressure to find less costly approaches
that meet broad customer needs with minimal complexity in products

and processes. While the generic strategy of Ryanair can be denoted as a low-price strategy, this does not render much insight into the business model of the company.

The low-cost option is *per se* open to all existing airlines, and many already compete alongside Ryanair on price. However, Ryanair was among the first airline companies to mould its business platform to create a sustainable low-price business. Many unique business models are easy to communicate because they have a unique quality about them, that is, either a unique concept or value proposition. This is also the case for Ryanair. It is the 'no-service business model'. In fact, the business model is so well thought-through that even the arrogance and attitude of the top management matches the culture of the rest of the business. But they can make money in an industry that has been under pressure for several decades despite upwards trending demographic changes and rising globalization, and for this they deserve recognition. Ryanair's business model narrative is the story of a novel flying experience – irrespective of the attitude of the customer after the ordeal.

A much-applied example in the management literature is Toyota, in regard to management culture as well as quality control and logistics systems. However, Toyota did not really change the value proposition – or the value chain – of the car industry. They were able to achieve superior quality through Just In Time (JIT) and lean management technologies, and they may have made slightly smaller cars than the American car producers, but their value proposition and operating platform were otherwise unchanged. The same can be said for Ford in the early 20th century. Ford's business setup was not really a new business model. It sold one car model in one colour, but so did most other car manufacturers at the time. Ford was able to reduce costs through a unique organization of the production setup, but the value proposition was not unique.

In the 1990s, Dell changed the personal computer industry by applying the Internet as a novel distribution channel. This platform as a foundation of the pricing strategy took out several parts of the sales channel, leaving a larger cut to Dell and cheaper personal computers to customers. Nowadays this distribution strategy is not a unique business model, as many other laptop producers apply it. Therefore, it also exemplifies that what is unique today is not necessarily unique tomorrow.

This mirrors Christensen's quote that "today's competitive advantage becomes tomorrow's albatross" (Christensen, 2001, p. 105). Having the right business model at the present does not necessarily guarantee success for years on end as new technology or changes in the business environment and customer base can influence profitability. The point to be made here is that if the value proposition is not affected in some manner, then it is most likely not a new business model. However, it could be the case that the value proposition is not affected, but the business' value-generating attributes are radically different from those of the competitors. Three examples of this are as follows.

1 The value proposition of two companies producing kitchen appliances. One may be more high-end than the other, but this is a part of the competitive strategy, not the actual business model.
2 The value proposition of two companies producing laptops. One may be priced lower because the range is smaller and the design kept to one colour. This is not only equivalent to different business models but also a question of competitive strategy and customer selection. However, if one of the producers decides to alter the traditional distribution model, cutting out store placement and setting up technical support as local franchisees only, that could be a new business model.
3 Two hair salons will both be performing haircuts, but their value propositions may be vastly different according to the physical setup around the core attribute – the haircut – in the form of booking services, physical attributes of the salon and its geographic placement as well as service before and after the haircut.

Business model conceptualized as building blocks: moving towards a dynamic perspective

While value creation from a typical financially oriented business perspective merely constitutes the realization of value at the time of sale of the product, that is, registration of turnover, from a process perspective value creation may be characterized as what happens inside the company before this financial value realization takes place. In this genre, we are more concerned with value creation potential, value creation processes and value creation extraction, all of which can be said to precede the value realization phase.

In 2002 Chesbrough and Rosenbloom tried to corner the important aspects to be considered to comprehensively describe the business model of the company. They defined the business model as a construct that integrates activities into a coherent framework. This definition is worth highlighting because it was among the first to set value creation as a central notion of understanding the points of concern in the business model of a company. In the wake of this definition, Chesbrough and Rosenbloom defined the six steps to creating a business model:

1   Articulate the value proposition, that is, the value created for users by the offering based on the technology.
2   Identify a market segment, that is, the users to whom the technology is useful and for what purpose.
3   Define the structure of the value chain within the firm required to create and distribute the offering.
4   Estimate the cost structure and profit potential of producing the offering, given the value proposition and value chain structure chosen.
5   Describe the position of the firm within the value network linking suppliers and customers, including identification of potential complementarities and competitors.
6   Formulate the competitive strategy by which the innovating firm will gain and hold advantage over rivals.

Zott and Amit's (2010) earlier quote on activity systems value capture is concerned with the balance between what is inside the financial boundary of a focal firm and what is outside, and how these are adjusted to displace costs and expenses and secure an additional margin. How much margin the focal firm captures from its total value chain depends upon its pricing strategy, pricing power, relation to distributors and retail network and capacity to outsource and offshore – that is, to what extent a focal firm has sufficient power benefit from price control, customer lock-in and ability to adjust internal and external cost structure through flexibility and/or synergies. As Zott and Amit (2010) observe, the "business model co-determines the focal firm's bargaining power", and this facilitates value capture out of its value-creating initiatives. Thus, business models are conceptualized, in general, as how focal firms' resources are deployed for value-creating products and services are located within a partnership network that secures revenue flows and determines cost structure. Hedman and Kalling (2003) propose that a generic business model is composed of causally related components: customers, competitors, the company offering (generic strategy), activities and organization (including the value chain), resources (human, physical and organizational) and factor and production inputs. Other authors offer insight on the most relevant building blocks (Baden-Fuller and Haefliger, 2013; Chesbrough and Rosenbloom, 2002; Demil and Lecocq, 2010; Hamel, 2000; Stähler,

2002). For example, Stähler (2002) proposes the following building blocks: the value proposition, the product or service, the value architecture and the revenue model.

Remembering that a business model – at least at an SBU level – may be perceived as a platform that enables the strategic choices within reach of a firm's management team to become profitable, it also becomes clear that a business model is neither merely a pricing strategy, a new distribution channel or an IT, nor is it a quality control scheme in the production setup. That is to say, none of the above actions are by themselves sufficient. Rather, a business model is concerned with the value proposition of the company, but it is not the value proposition alone, as it is in itself supported by a number of parameters and characteristics – for example, some of the parameters mentioned earlier, like applied distribution channels, customer relationships, pricing models and sourcing from strategic partnerships. One of the major questions to answer in relation to understanding business models is, therefore, how is the strategy and value proposition of the company aligned and leveraged?

The problem with trying to visualize the 'business model' through separate building blocks is that it can very quickly become a generic and static organization-like diagram illustrating the process of transforming inputs to outputs in a chain-like fashion. The reader is thus more often than not left wondering how the organization actually functions. Hence, the core of the business model description should be the connections between the different elements that an organizational diagram or value chain traditionally depicts, that is, the actual activities being performed in the company. Companies often communicate a lot of information about activities, such as customer relationships, varying distribution channels, employee competencies, knowledge sharing activities, innovation and risks, but this information may seem unimportant if the company fails to show how these various elements of value creation collaborate between one another and which changes the management team will be monitoring. One such idea on how to visualize the business model is the popular Business Model Canvas by Osterwalder and Pigneur (2010) (Figure 14).

When we perceive relationships and linkages, they often reflect some kind of tangible transactions, that is, the flow of products, services or money. When perceiving and analyzing the value transactions going on inside an organization, or between an organization and its partners, there is a marked tendency to neglect or forget the parallel intangible transactions and interrelations that are also

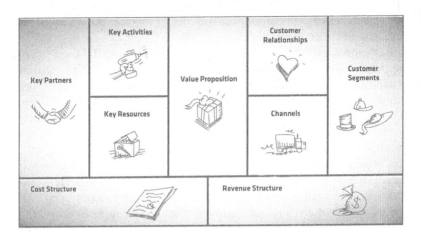

Figure 14 The Business Model Canvas (adapted from Osterwalder and Pigneur, 2010; see www.businessmodelgeneration.com).

involved. This is supported in Osterwalder and Pigneur's framework (2010) and is probably one reason why their book has sold so many copies to date.

Alt and Zimmermann (2001) discuss these aspects by way of the concept of the value proposition, which they perceive as a (customer centric) part of the company's mission statement together with its vision and strategic goals. Chesbrough and Rosenbloom (2002) similarly define the value proposition as the value created for the user of the company's offering, while Hedman and Kalling (2003) have a slightly different perception of the value proposition as the generic strategy of the company. In Osterwalder *et al.* (2005), the value proposition towards customer segments plays a vital role in the configuration of a business model and in their book, discussing the "Value Proposition Canvas" tool (Osterwalder *et al.*, 2014). Osterwalder and Pigneur strengthen the articulation between their Business Model Canvas and Steve Blank's (2013) work on customer needs, best reflected in his book *Four Steps to the Epiphany* (Blank, 2013).[2]

Business model archetypes and patterns

Business model archetypes and patterns have been an area of focus in the field of business models since its emergence in the late 1990s (Bell *et al.*, 1997; Timmers, 1998). Among the state of the art research within this particular stream is the work coming out of Oliver Gassmann's research group at St. Gallen University (see Frankenberger *et al.*, 2013; Gassmann *et al.*, 2014), Colin Haslam's research unit at Queen Mary University (Andersson *et al.*, 2014; Haslam *et al.*, 2013) and Christian Nielsen's Business Design Center at Aalborg University (Taran *et al.*, 2016). In general, this research on business model archetypes is concerned with finding categorizations that make benchmarking and innovation of business models easier.

Baden-Fuller and Morgan (2010) take on the discussion of business models conceptualized as models of reality. Representation is essentially modelling, as it concerns creating images of reality. Thus, images of the outside world are projected to us through representation (via, for example, some sort of 'technology', that is, a business model or other management technology). Cooper (1992) and Latour (1999) ask whether the world outside is different from the one we have in here. Latour argues that representation becomes reality as it is a construction of objectivity. From his point of view, interaction is the essence of existence. Through interaction, objects become real only when they are circulatable. He develops this argument by stating that 3D objects – unlike 2D objects – cannot be circulated, in a sense arguing that representation is reality (Latour, 1999). In this case representation abbreviates complexity (Zuboff, 1988, pp. 179–180).

Cooper (1992) concludes that representation is the transformation of the object – in our case the company – into a new form that produces controllability. Furthermore, influenced by Zuboff (1988), he argues for three underlying themes of representation; these constitute the mechanisms by which representation realizes this economy of mental and physical motion being remote control, displacement and abbreviation.

Through remote control, symbols and other devices substitute for direct involvement with and between people – in organizations the employees and management. Remote control thus underlines an economy of convenience by enabling control at a distance. The power of representation is the ability to control an event remotely and can be described as a form of displacement in which representation is always a substitution for or representation of the event, and never the event itself. The mobility of representation, created through displacement, is central to control (and thereby also to power). Displacement emerges either as a transformation of the object, or as conceptual or material mobility, for example, via projection. Displacement denotes mobile and non-localizable associations, while abbreviation makes possible the economy of convenience that underlies representation. Abbreviation, inducing a subset of the original object, is a principle of condensation, which enables ease and accuracy of perception and action. Through abbreviation, representations are made compact, versatile and permutable. Hence the conclusion of this section is that there are interesting avenues for further research that connects the notions of models, representation, stories and communication. However, these aspects of theorization are not at the core of the present book.

One of the specific business model typologies that was created with the advent of e-business was the digital platform, and the recent literature (Frankenberger *et al.*, 2013; Gassmann *et al.*, 2014; Taran *et al.*, 2016) illustrates a number of business model patterns based on platform thinking. Brousseau and Penard (2007) analyze the economics of matching, the economics of assembling and the economics of knowledge management in relation to platform thinking and attempt to identify the principal trade-offs at the core of choices among alternative digital business models, and to compare them in terms of competitiveness and efficiency. No optimal model can be identified at any one time, but models that result in the best practical compromise between the specific nature of the assembled goods, the disparity and nature of users' preferences, production constraints faced by the function provider (level of costs, share of fixed costs in total costs, etc.), and the structure of competition between platforms.

An archetype can be defined as a typical example of something, or the original model of something from which others are copied. According to Taran *et al.* (2016), the psychologist Carl Jung (1875–1961) was one of the first to introduce the term archetypes and argued that "All the most powerful ideas in history go back to archetypes. This is particularly true of religious ideas, but the central concepts of science, philosophy, and ethics are no exception to this rule" (Jung, 1927, p. 342). The study of archetypes has expanded over the years into other research disciplines such as biology, neurology, ethology and pedagogy (see, for example, Mayes, 2010; Samuels *et al.*, 1986), and there has been a growing interest in trying to identify successful business models across different industries (see, for example, Linder and Cantrell, 2000; Osterwalder and Pigneur, 2010).

As is evident from the earlier discussions, many authors have attempted to define business models by discussing and identifying overall business model generics and archetypes. In 1998, Timmers had already classified ten generic types of Internet business models; two years later, Rappa (2001) identified 41 types of Internet business models and classified them into nine categories. In recent years, it is increasingly being realized that archetypes of e-business in reality might merely be translations of already existing business models. And thus, business model archetypes seen through today's lens could be something along the lines of

* buyer–seller models;
* advanced buyer–seller models;
* network-based business models;
* multisided business models;
* business models based on ecology;
* BoP business models;
* business models based on social communities;
* co-creation and consumer-collaboration models;
* freemium models.

In particular, identifying these archetypes suggests that business models work like 'recipes' that could be generalized to develop successful businesses (Pateli and Giaglis, 2004). In other words, business model archetypes are ideal examples that describe and distinguish the behaviour of companies operating in the real world, thus providing managers, practitioners and academics with recipes that have already been tried and tested (Fielt, 2014). Just like recipes, business model archetypes describe the 'ingredients' to use as well as the process by which these ingredients are mixed to obtain the final dish, that is, a successful business model. Despite the relevance of this stream, systematic research in business model archetypes is still limited, as there is a lack of knowledge on the conceptual foundations of what a successful business model should look like.

A variety of labels have been used to identify business model archetypes. Linder and Cantrell (2000) coin the expression 'operating business model' by highlighting 33 different formats. Johnson (2010) pinpoints 19 possible business model configurations, using the term 'analogies', while Osterwalder and Pigneur (2010) exploit the term 'patterns' by drawing attention to five business model templates: unbundling business model; long tail; multi-sided platforms; freemium; and open business model.

Despite the different terminologies used to frame business model archetypes, the underlining aims are common across different authors: identifying and describing business models with similar features, dynamics or behaviours to make them comparable, easy to understand and applicable. Business model archetypes are often labelled with the names of specific real-life companies, which are supposed to frame particular strong points and specific features, like the 'McDonald's business model' or the 'eBay business model'. Thus, some archetypes are descriptions of real-life businesses, while others can be considered more generic conceptualizations of a particular real-world business model, like the 'franchising business model' or the 'e-auction business model'.

This different way of labelling business model archetypes involves two conceptions of models, that is, scale models and role models; the former provides brief descriptions of business models of real companies that compete on the market, while the latter offers general ideal cases that work in a particular way (Baden-Fuller and Morgan, 2010). Archetypes are ready-to-use templates that can be copied by other companies, even with minor variations in the 'ingredients' or in the mixing process, but without changing the basic recipe. Identifying archetypes suggests there are several ways by which companies can achieve success, but also many generic types and many possible changes within each of them can be identified. All in all, business model archetypes are practical frameworks, which are ready for copying but also for modifications and innovations, thus entailing opportunities to open up further developments.

Transformative redefinition: relevant second stage business model research paths

- Business model researchers need to specifically address our lack of understanding of the levers and the barriers to business model innovation and business model implementation, and possibly identifying decision-support systems for business model innovation processes and business model implementation processes in order for these practices to spread to the wider array of SMEs in the economy. While business models spark a natural interest among entrepreneurs and SMEs, researchers have not yet addressed the challenges such organizations will face in meeting a very complex and seemingly all-inclusive conceptualization of firms' value creation. In addition to decision-support studies, research should reach out to the SME segment for cases to ground future theorizing.
- In accordance with Wirtz *et al.* (2016b), we argue that research should aim at consolidating and confirming existing business model frameworks empirically.
- Finally, linking business models with notions of sustainability and more socially fair dispersions of value is an important avenue to pursue in terms of validating the consequences of sustainability and non-sustainability.

Notes

1 Interestingly, the notion of business model innovation patterns is also deeply rooted in the most cited piece of work in the third stage of business model research, namely Osterwalder and Pigneur's (2010) *Business Model Generation*, but has not been theorized about until recently by Gassmann *et al.* (2014) and Taran *et al.* (2016).

2 The relationships among business model components will be properly addressed in the third stage of business model research. Conceptualizing business models as complex systems (Foss and Saebi, 2017) allows one to consider the interdependencies and the interactions among the components. See also Baden-Fuller and Haefliger (2013).

7 Third stage business model research

Design frameworks and foundations for theory-building

The third stage of business model research is dominated by a special issue in *Long Range Planning* (Volume 43, Issues 2–3) that aims to clarify the links between the concept of business models and related fields (argued as missing in stage 1 research) but also outlines the contours for future theorizing in the field. In addition to these contributions, some literature reviews are carried out (Foss and Saebi, 2017; Lambert and Davidson, 2013; Massa *et al.*, 2017; Schneider and Spieth, 2013) to take stock of the extant literature of the first and second stage, lay the foundations for theory-building and offer suggestions for future research. Moreover, within the third stage, frameworks for describing, designing and innovating business models are proposed. The work typically undertaken in this stage of research focuses on private sector firms, while public sector research is almost non-existent. A number of research streams that may be connected to this stage of research are found in the current literature.

Clarifying the business model foundations

Contributions within the third stage start to investigate the theoretical underpinnings of the business model concept. Before the third stage, not much attention was paid to the issue of theory (Morris *et al.*, 2005); a lot has been written about business models, but the lack of a well-defined theoretical foundation has led to inconsistent empirical findings, thus inhibiting cumulative research progress (Bock *et al.*, 2012; Zott *et al.*, 2011). A notable exception can be found in Amit and Zott (2001), who, in 2001, faced this issue by framing the business model as a unifying concept able to capture value from multiple sources. The authors explore the business model concept from several theoretical stances, that is, the value chain framework (Porter, 1985), Schumpeter's theory of creative destruction (Schumpeter, 1942), the resource-based view of the firm (e.g. Barney, 1991), strategic network theory (e.g. Dyer and Singh, 1998), and transaction costs economics (Williamson, 1975). Based on this analysis, Amit and Zott (2001) argued for a cross-theoretical perspective, as no single theory, *per se*, can explain the value creation potential that lies within the business model concept.

Morris *et al.* (2005) find that the business model holds promise as a unifying unit of analysis that can facilitate theory development in entrepreneurship, which is more recently highlighted by George and Bock (2011). Morris *et al.* (2005) explore the theoretical underpinnings of a firm's business model and agree with Amit and Zott (2001) in regard to the cross-theoretical anchoring of the business model concept. However, these authors add some theoretical lenses that can be helpful to interpret the business model concept:

- value systems and strategic positioning (Porter, 1996), as the choice of the position within the value system is critical for the sake of value creation;
- systems theory (von Bertalanffy, 1951), that allows conceptualization of the business model as "interrelated components of a system that constitutes the firm's architectural backbone" (Morris *et al.*, 2005, p. 729).

Within the concept of the business model, the value chain may be said to comprise a company's activities (Hedman and Kalling, 2003) and structure (Alt and Zimmermann, 2001). Hence there are, at least, some connections with, for example, Osterwalder and Pigneur's (2010) Business Model Canvas. The concept of modelling the organization, that is, creating organization charts, analyzing how departments and divisions interact with and affect each other and optimization of the whole enterprise as opposed to suboptimization, thereby creating an overview and easing the understanding of how it functions is not a new concept. Management teams, consultants and academics alike have been doing this for ages.

Like the value chain, a business model is the company's underlying structure, but the business model goes further, because it also describes the underlying concept, or method, of value creation, which ultimately leads to profits and long-term sustainability. Technology is not to be underestimated within the business model concept, as it is a key element in determining which organizational structures become profitable and can be realized (Kraemer *et al.*, 1999). Among the seminal contributions with respect to technology's impact on the feasibility of business model concepts is Thompson's *Organizations in Action* (1967). Thompson proposes a typology of different kinds of organizational technologies, distinguishing between long-linked, intensive and mediating technologies (see also Stabell and Fjeldstad, 1998). These different technology types play different roles in connection with value creation and thus also structuring of companies and their value chains. Changes in the business landscape and technologies for interaction affect a broad range of industries and are not restricted to relevance to e-business. For example, Chapman *et al.* (2002) illustrate how entering into the knowledge society has changed the competitive prerequisites of the logistics industry. Their research concludes that the rising application of IT has changed the ingredients of survival and partnering, and thereby the business model of that industry.

More recently, a special issue in *Long Range Planning* (Volume 43, Issues 2–3) tried to define the theoretical profile of the business model concept. Teece (2010) argues that the business model is an interdisciplinary topic lacking a theoretical anchoring in economics or business studies. By assuming that markets are perfect, economic theory underplays the relevance of business model factors, such as the mechanisms to capture value, the fit between value proposition and customer segments or the choice of a suitable channel. Organizational, strategic and marketing science flag the importance of the business model concept, but fail to analyze it properly and to provide it a theoretical home; as a result, the business model is frequently mentioned but poorly understood.

Zott and Amit (2010) conceptualize the business model as a system of interdependent activities that transcends focal firm and spans its boundaries. By drawing on activity theory, the authors underscore the relevance of the architecture of a company's activity system (the choice of the activities to perform, the relationships among activities, the actors who perform the activities). The design of this architecture also helps define the role played by the company within its ecosystem, that is, its network of customers, partners and suppliers.

By adopting a Penrosian perspective (Penrose, 1959), Demil and Lecocq (2010) position themselves among those who trace back the theoretical foundations of business models within the resource-based view of the firm (Teece, 1984; Wernerfelt, 1984); the competitive advantage of a company depends on its rare, unique and non-substitutable resources, as well as on management's ability to extract value from them.

Schneider and Spieth (2013) provide an overview of the theoretical lenses that can be used to interpret the business model concept. In particular, the authors take into consideration three theoretical perspective that analyze the business model from a different angle.

1 **The resource-based view**. In accordance with previous research (e.g. Amit and Zott, 2001; Demil and Lecocq, 2010), the authors acknowledge that this theoretical perspective for research on business models is fruitful, as it traces back the heterogeneity among firms to the resources at their disposal (Teece, 1984; Wernerfelt, 1984) as well as to the managerial actions to use these resources (Helfat *et al.*, 2007; Sirmon *et al.*, 2007). Both these elements emphasize the relevance of the business model in coordinating the company's resources for the sake of achieving a competitive advantage.

2 **The dynamic-capabilities perspective**, which underscores the constant need of companies to reinvent themselves by applying new value creation strategies (Grant, 1996; Pisano, 1994) in view of the hyper-competitive and global business environment, thus implicitly underlining the relevance of business model innovation.

3 **The strategic entrepreneurship perspective**, which is the "integration of entrepreneurial (i.e. opportunity-seeking behaviour) and strategic (i.e. advantage-seeking) perspectives" for the purpose of creating value (Hitt *et al.*, 2001, 480). By including all forms of innovations aimed at exploring and exploiting new opportunities, this theoretical framework is suitable to conduct research on business models when it comes to changing established ways of doing business (Amit and Zott, 2010).

Finally, Foss and Saebi (2017) argue that complexity theory can be a fruitful theoretical framework to analyze the business model concept. Such a view conceptualizes the business model as a complex system (Simon, 1962, 1973), meaning that the business model is composed of a series of interdependent and complementary subsystems (value creation, value delivery and value capture) that interact in a non-simple way. Complex systems can be categorized according to the degree of interdependency among subsystems:

1 highly modular systems, interactions are negligible;
2 non-decomposable systems, interactions are essential;
3 nearly decomposable systems, interactions are weak, but not negligible.

According to the type of complex system, the effects of innovation are different. Innovating a highly modular business model may entail only changes in one or more subsystems, while no architectural change (i.e. the relationships among subsystems) may be required. On the contrary, if a business model is a non-decomposable system, the effects of innovation are likely to involve not only one or more subsystems, but overall a deep redesign of the architecture of the business model itself.

Business model ecosystems

Business models are designed and implemented in specific environments, which can influence or be influenced by the business models (Osterwalder and Pigneur, 2010). Considering the ecosystems in which the business models operate allows managers and practitioners to build more competitive and consistent business models and it permits academics to obtain a broader perspective on the business model research area.

Regarding business model ecosystems, Osterwalder and Pigneur (2010) identify four main elements:

1   market forces (market issues, market segments, needs and demands, switching costs, revenues attractiveness);
2   industry forces (competitors, new entrants, substitute products, suppliers and other value chain actors, stakeholders);
3   key trends (technology trends, regulatory trends, societal and cultural trends, socio economic trends); and
4   macroeconomic forces (global market conditions, capital markets, commodities and other resources, economic infrastructure).

Zott and Amit (2013, p. 407) acknowledge the relevance of the ecosystem concept from a business model perspective; the authors indeed recognize "the need to go beyond a focal firm's boundaries and adopt a more systemic perspective that emphasizes interdependencies and complementarities between a firm and third parties to properly understand how value is created".

The ecosystem concept allows Sanchez and Ricart (2010) to classify business models in two categories:

1   **isolated business models**, which pursue exploitation strategies, the company's resources and capabilities are leveraged to achieve efficiency; and
2   **interactive business models**, which adopt exploration strategies, the company's internal resources are integrated with external ones to foster innovation processes and the creation of new market opportunities.

Mapping the business model's ecosystem current features and reflecting upon the future trends of external forces are very relevant activities because they trigger thoughts on potential changes and innovations to improve the current business model. Indeed, a business model could be strong and consistent in the current competitive landscape, but it could rapidly become obsolete because of technology innovations or new disruptive value propositions. To sum up, the business model should evolve at the same pace as the ecosystem in which it is deployed. Despite the relevance of this stream, how the business model ecosystems influence the evolution (see also Leblebici, 2012) and the dynamics of business models and vice versa are still areas open for research.[1]

The need for taxonomies of business models

Classifying objects in homogenous categories is a very relevant activity within a research domain as it allows researchers to organize abstract and complex concepts (Neuman, 2003), thus triggering further insights to advance research in a certain domain. As Bailey (1994, p. 15) states, "Theory cannot explain much if it is based on an inadequate system of classification". In the business model research domain, categorization is possibly a powerful tool as it makes possible the positioning of business model archetypes close to each other based on underlying criteria, thus increasing the understanding of the business model research area and enabling the development of ideal types (Baden-Fuller and Morgan, 2010). Figure 15 shows Osterwalder

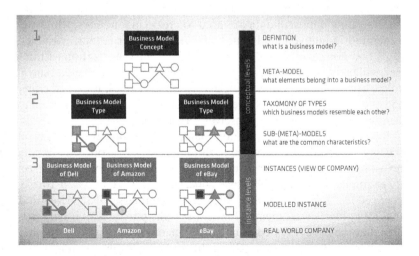

Figure 15 The relationship between business model archetypes and categories (adapted from Osterwalder *et al.*, 2005).

et al.'s conceptions of the relationships between business model archetypes and categories.

As shown by Lambert and Davidson (2013), the business model is increasingly used as criteria to categorize homogeneous groups of companies. Business-model-based classifications provide a new angle from which to analyze industries and, moreover, can be the starting point for other management studies (e.g. investigating the performance of different classes of business models). The path towards theorizing strongly relies on the opportunity to classify objects and on the quality of the categorization system; as Bailey (1994, p. 15) states, "theory cannot explain much if it is based on an inadequate system of classification", and business model research is not an exception. As a matter of fact, generalizations about categories of business models require a classification scheme able to identify homogeneous categories of business models and to make it possible the comparison between heterogeneous classes (Baden-Fuller and Morgan, 2010; Lambert and Montemari, 2017).

When it comes to classifying objects in homogeneous groups, two options are possible: typologies and taxonomies (Doty and Glick, 1994). Typologies are designed in a deductive manner and consider only few variables to define the classes of objects; intuition and/or existing theories are used to craft the classes, which are only useful for very specific purposes (i.e. the immediate needs of researchers), while revealing themselves to be of limited usefulness when it comes to other purposes. Following along these lines, it can be argued that typologies provide a basis for only limited generalizations. In contrast, statistical analysis and empirical data are used to create taxonomies, which are generated inductively and simultaneously consider several variables. Only taxonomies can enable generalizations and theorization within a particular research field. Either way, empirical research plays a central role when it comes to building classification schemes; it is used either to validate conceptually derived categories (typologies) or it is used to determine the categories themselves (taxonomies).

Business model research is dominated by typological classification schemes; several arbitrary categorizations have been proposed, making no explicit reference to, or using only a few, classification criteria (see, for example, Bambury, 1998; Betz, 2002; Chen, 2003; Dubosson-Torbay *et al.*, 2002; Mäkinen and Seppänen, 2007; Timmers, 1998). Given that these typologies were created for very specific purposes, it is only natural that they are revealed to be mostly inconsistent with one another (Lambert, 2015; Taran *et al.*, 2016). In contrast, taxonomical research is scant; the lack of a taxonomical classification scheme is a significant gap for business model research as it considerably limits the progress towards generalizations on homogeneous groups of business models as well as the development of business model theories (Groth and Nielsen, 2015; Lambert, 2015; Lambert and Montemari, 2017; Mäkinen and Seppänen, 2007).

Business model archetypes, which present common features, can be classified in abstract categories (Fielt, 2014; Osterwalder *et al.*, 2005); in a sense, if archetypes are the 'recipes', categories can be considered the 'recipe book'. Other authors have made some attempts to identify business model categorizations without clarifying the criteria used to differentiate business model archetypes (Applegate, 2001; Bambury, 1998; Eisenmann, 2002; Laudon and Traver, 2003). As for business model definitions, frameworks and archetypes, business model classifications are also very heterogeneous as there is little integration of criteria and dimensions used by the different authors to categorize business model archetypes (Fielt, 2014; Lambert, 2006). Even though researchers and practitioners have been highlighting the need for a generally accepted business model categorization (Hawkins, 2002; Keen and Qureshi, 2006; Pateli and Giaglis, 2004), the state of the art in this business model research stream is still unable to provide exhaustive answers.

Moreover, when business model categorization comes up for discussion, the distinction between specific classifications (typologies) and generic classifications (taxonomies) has to be addressed (McKelvey, 1982). Table 5 shows the features and the functions of typologies and taxonomies.

Regarding this distinction, none of the aforementioned business model classifications can be considered taxonomies, as they are created to pursue the particular aims of the researchers and they cannot be exploited for multiple purposes. Even though these typologies have

Table 5 Features and functions of typologies and taxonomies

Typologies	Taxonomies
Categories (types) are conceptually derived	Categories (taxa) are empirically derived
Few characteristics considered	Many characteristics considered
Reasoning by deduction	Reasoning by inference
Mostly qualitative classifications	Quantitative classifications
Specific/arbitrary/artificial classification	General/natural classification
Provides a basis for only limited generalizations	Provides a basis for generalization

Source: Adapted from Lambert (2006).

contributed to shedding new light on the nature and the role of business models, by simplifying such a complex domain and identifying relationships between a small number of variables, they are not able to provide a generally accepted nomenclature of business models. All in all, the aforementioned typologies help to achieve parsimony, but they are limited in terms of versatility. This aim can be achieved using statistical analysis to build taxonomies from a large number of variables to be considered simultaneously (Lambert, 2006).

Designing frameworks for describing, designing and innovating business models

Zott and Amit (2010, p. 217) observe that "given the vital importance of the business model for entrepreneurs and general managers, it is surprising that academic research (with a few exceptions) has so far devoted little attention to this topic". Further, they argue that "we need a conceptual toolkit that enables entrepreneurial managers to design their future business model, as well as to help managers analyze and improve their current designs to make them fit for the future" (Zott and Amit, 2010, p. 217). A notable exception can be found in Morris *et al.* (2005), who synthesize a six-component framework for characterizing a business model, regardless of venture type. These six components (factors related to the offering, market factors, internal capability factors, competitive strategy factors, economic factors, personal/investor factors), they argue, can be viewed on a foundational level. Additionally, two other levels exist, namely the proprietary level, which is concerned with the creation of unique combinations of components, and finally, the level of rules, which is concerned with establishing guiding principles for business model configuration.

Casadesus-Masanell and Zhu (2013), Schneider and Spieth (2013) and Spieth *et al.* (2014) also highlight that the process of business model innovation deserves additional analysis, concerning the design of tools and methods to support managers and practitioners to actually execute it. In view of this gap, some frameworks for describing, designing and innovating the business model are proposed within the third stage.

Demil and Lecocq (2010) assume that the business model concept is based on the interaction among three core components:

1   resources (bought externally or developed internally) and competences (abilities and knowledge of managers in improving the way in which resources are used);

2 organizational structure, that is, the value chain of activities and the value network (the relations with external stakeholders); and
3 value propositions that a company delivers to its customers.

The Business Model Canvas proposed by Osterwalder and Pigneur (2010) has gained in popularity among business developers, entrepreneurs and academics alike because it provides a shared language to describe, visualize and assess companies' business models, bringing together the different building blocks for a complete understanding of the business model. Osterwalder and Pigneur (2010) argue that a business model can be described through nine basic building blocks that show the logic of how a company intends to make money. The nine blocks cover the four main areas of a business:

1 customer interface (customer segments, channels, customer relationships);
2 products and services (value proposition);
3 infrastructure (key activities, key resources, key partnerships); and
4 financial viability (revenue streams, cost structure).

Eyring *et al.* (2011) are exponents of a recent customer centric school of thought in the business model literature. In their study of business configurations in emerging markets (see also Pitelis, 2009) they argue that a good business model starts with understanding customers. Using Peter Drucker's quote, "The customer rarely buys what the business thinks it sells him", the following recipe is provided.

1 Study what your customers are doing with your product.
2 Look at the alternatives to your offerings that consumers buy. Investigate a wide range of substitutes for your products, not just what your competitors make.
3 Watch for compensating behaviours. Discover what jobs people are satisfying poorly.
4 Search for explanations. Uncover the root causes of consumers' behaviour by asking what people are trying to accomplish with the goods and services they use.

This type of methodology is widespread in some of the customer-insight and design-thinking-based entrepreneurship research relating to opportunity spotting and customer intelligence and provides a neat link between the field of business models, new venture creation and design-thinking.

Gassmann *et al.* (2014) present the Business Model Navigator, a framework to help companies innovate their business model. The Business Model Navigator assumes that successful business models can be built by creatively imitating business models from other industries. To gain inspiration from what already exists, the Navigator presents an impressive list of 55 various business model patterns (according to their terminology), which covers 90% of business model innovation possibilities. Each pattern is analyzed based on a four-dimensional framework addressing the value proposition (what?), value chain (how?), profit mechanism (why?) and target customer (who?).

Taran *et al.* (2016) develop the 5-V framework, aimed at facilitating companies in innovating their business model. The framework includes a toolbox of 71 business model patterns (or business model configurations, according to their terminology) from which companies can choose to innovate their business model. These business model patterns are classified within five categories.

1   **Value Proposition**: it concerns the company's offering and the features for which customers are willing to pay for (e.g. uniqueness, customization, convenience, brand status, reliability).
2   **Value Segment**: it is the segment of customers that a company targets. It also includes the type of relationships that a company establishes with its customers (e.g. lock-in, co-creation, self-service).
3   **Value Configuration**: it includes the mix of key resources needed and the key activities performed to create the value proposition as well as the channels used to deliver the value proposition to the target segment. The costs that a company incurs to configure and deliver value are also included in this dimension.
4   **Value Network**: it includes the network of partners who can cooperate with a company, with the goal of achieving mutual benefits (risk reduction, cost reduction, accessing a particular customer segment, accessing a new key resource).
5   **Value Capture**: it describes how much customers pay to obtain the value proposition, that is, the share of the value created that a company is able to capture. It also includes the different means that a company can use to capture value (e.g. commission, leasing, auction, subscription).

The 5-V framework assumes that every real-life company is a combination of different business model configurations, linked to the five distinct dimensions.

Towards a consistent perspective on business model innovation

Within the third stage, a number of literature reviews on business models and business model innovation are carried out to take stock of the extant literature of the first and second stage and to define future avenues of research.

Lambert and Davidson (2013) perform a literature review of the research field of business models from 1996 and 2010. Consistent with the content of Chapter 4, three main themes emerge from their analysis:

1   business model as a criterion to classify companies;
2   business model as a driver of performance; and
3   business model innovation.

Within the theme of business model innovation, two sub-themes surface:

1   the reasons that push companies to innovate their business model are basically external factors (de Reuver *et al.*, 2009), such as a hypercompetitive environment or industry transformation, and internal factors (Giesen *et al.*, 2010), such as new product or service offerings, or open innovation opportunities (Chesbrough, 2006), to capture the benefits of knowledge sharing;
2   the factors that drive the successful innovation of the business model, such as the ability to monitor innovations through sophisticated analytics (Giesen *et al.*, 2010) or the ability to continuously reassess and modify the business model to suit changing conditions (Sosna *et al.*, 2010).

In the attempt to provide a complete overview of the extant literature and to identify prevalent patterns, Schneider and Spieth (2013) conduct a systematic literature review on publications from 1981 and 2012. The analysis shows three main streams of research within business model innovation:

1   prerequisites, such as the globalization of the business environment (Lee *et al.*, 2012) or massive technological changes (Wirtz *et al.*, 2010);
2   process and elements, where business model innovation has been conceptualized as a continuous reaction to changes (Demil and Lecocq, 2010), an ongoing learning process (Sosna *et al.*, 2010),

an evolutionary process (Dunford *et al.*, 2010), a trial-and-error-based process (McGrath, 2010); and

3   effects, where three sub-streams have been identified: (i) effects on the industry logics (e.g. Casadesus-Masanell and Zhu, 2013; Sabatier *et al.*, 2012); (ii) effects on individual company performance (e.g. Aspara *et al.*, 2010; Hall and Wagner, 2012); (iii) effects on individual company's capabilities, such as strategic flexibility (e.g. Bock *et al.*, 2010).

Foss and Saebi (2017) conduct a literature review on business model innovation by analyzing 150 peer-reviewed papers published between 2000 and 2015. Consistent with Schneider and Spieth (2013), the authors identify four relevant streams of research in business model innovation:

1   understanding business model innovation, that is, offering definitions and identifying the dimensions of the business model that can be innovated;
2   analyzing the process of business model innovation, that is, identifying stages, organizational capabilities needed, proposing tools to execute the process;
3   examining the outcome of the business model innovation, that is, focusing on the features of the new and innovative business model arising from the process of business model innovation;
4   investigating the effects of business model innovation, that is, facing the performance implications of business model innovation.

Despite Foss and Saebi (2017) recognizing that these four streams have helped advance our understanding of the nature, process and effects of this phenomenon, these authors also acknowledge that research on business model innovation "does not exhibit the characteristics of a well-defined cumulative research stream" (p. 208); contributions are conceptual rather than theoretical or descriptive rather than explanatory. Moreover, the four research streams have evolved separately and do not support each other in the process of cumulative growth of knowledge. To advance business model innovation research, Foss and Saebi (2017)

•   define business model innovation as "designed, novel, and non-trivial changes to the key elements of a firm's business model and/ or the architecture linking these elements" (p. 216);
•   provide a business innovation typology, based on the novelty and scope of the innovation itself, which leads to the identification

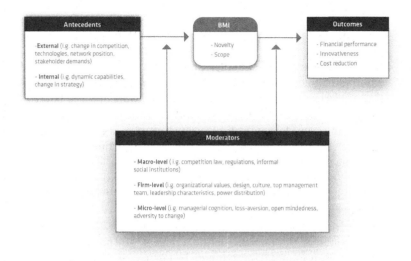

Figure 16 Extension of Foss and Saebi's (2017) business model innovation research framework.

of four types of business model innovation with well-defined features – evolutionary, focused, adaptive, complex; and
• create a research framework that clarifies where business model innovation is situated in terms of antecedent, moderating, mediating and outcome variables.

Figure 16 shows our elaboration from the research framework proposed by Foss and Saebi (2017):

Transformative redefinition: relevant third stage business model research paths

The relevant third stage business model research paths are as follows:

• From Critique 2 – extending the educational implications of business models to undiscovered contexts, such as public sector organizations and emerging markets, is an important research path to pursue.
• Following from this, and in accordance with Groth and Nielsen (2015), Lambert (2015) and Lambert and Montemari (2017), future

research should aim at empirically building taxonomies of business models and from these build business model archetypes as this would enable business model theory-building in the years to come.

- In accordance with Schneider and Spieth (2013) and Foss and Saebi (2017), we acknowledge that future research should investigate research questions like what are the levers and the barriers to the innovation of a business model? Under which conditions can business model innovation create a sustained competitive advantage? How can business model innovation surface? Exclusively from the top management or also from the lower levels of organization? It is worth noting that, given the nature of these research questions, it would be fruitful to investigate them from a performative perspective; and
- Future research should continue to investigate the theoretical foundations of the business model concept, so that research can progress in a cumulative manner. In particular, we find the perspective proposed by Foss and Saebi (2017), who conceptualize the business model as a complex system, very promising.

Note

1 It is worth noting that the origin of the ecosystem approach to business models can be traced back to the concepts of open innovation and open business models (Chesbrough, 2003, 2006).

8 Fourth stage business model research

The performative phase

Using 'heat maps' of the studies across topics and research questions, it is evident that the significant impact of Osterwalder and Pigneur's (2010) design-oriented Business Model Canvas marks the beginnings of research into entrepreneurship and start-ups (Doganova and Eyquem-Renault, 2009; George and Bock, 2011). Both Zott *et al.* (2011) and Wirtz *et al.* (2016b) argue that future business model research should focus on the financial aspects of the business model. Our analyses indicate that the performance of business models has been a stable theme in the field across all four stages depicted here; however, tests of how business model elements predict financial value are still lacking. Recently published research has started to address these notions (Nielsen *et al.*, 2017; Taran *et al.*, 2016), but it is too early yet to assess its impact. In this performative phase we would expect to see more dominant research addressing barriers to business model innovation, business model implementation, decision-support systems for business modelling processes and varying uses of the business model.

A business model is a way of doing business, perhaps closest understood as a concept for making money. A sustainable business would be a firm with the ambition to survive over time and create a successful, perhaps even profitable, entity in the long run. The reason for this apparent ambiguity around the concept of profitability is, of course, that business models apply to many different settings, not just the profit-oriented company. The application of business models is much broader and is a meaningful concept both in relation to public sector administration, NGOs, schools and universities and individuals. A recent contribution to this latter concept is the book *Business Model You* by Clark *et al.* (2012; see also Svejenova *et al.*, 2012), which translates the ideas of Osterwalder and Pigneur's (2010) Business Model Canvas into a personal setting for career enhancement purposes.

Whether profits are retained by shareholders or distributed in some degree to a broader mass of stakeholders, as in the case of the privately owned company, is not the focus here. Rather, it is the point of this book to illustrate how one may go about conceptualizing, analyzing or communicating the business model of a company, organization or person.

Verstraete and Jouison-Laffitte (2011) define the business model as a convention for value generation, value remuneration and the division of this remuneration among involved stakeholders in an entrepreneurial project. They argue that the business model is not a 'total' concept integrating all the aspects of firm foundation. Rather, it should propose a synthesis of the relations of value exchange by questioning their nature, their methods and their remuneration.

From a slightly different perspective, Fiet and Patel (2008) consider how the entrepreneurship that drives business model adaptation involves financial risk; a perspective also alluded to by Shi and Manning (2009). They argue that knowledge of the dependency of other partners within the business model could help to redistribute risk. The authors note that business model adaptations driven by entrepreneurs need to map out the possibility of risk displacement allowing "entrepreneurs to notice that resource providers have high market interaction costs and few outside options for negotiating a better deal with others" (Fiet and Patel, 2008, p. 759). Doganova and Eyquem-Renault (2009) study the role of business models in a start-up context and examine business models as market-oriented tools that entrepreneurs can apply to get from invention to customer needs and thus to innovation. They find that business models take varying forms, for example, from corporate presentations to business plans, and show that the business model plays a major role, not only as a narrative about value creation but also as a calculative device that allows entrepreneurs to explore a market and plays a performative role by contributing to the construction of the techno-economic network of an innovation. In the latter stream of literature relating to born global companies, there are also interesting contributions to understanding the internationalization of business models (Dunford *et al.*, 2010; Onetti *et al.*, 2012).

In his paper "Explicating dynamic capabilities: The nature and microfoundations of (sustainable) enterprise performance" Teece (2007) takes the vantage point of corporate sustainability from a resource-based perspective. It might be argued that sustainability, or should we say viability, would be equivalent to the ability to create sustainable profits and survive over time. Teece (2007) attempts to unveil the nature and microfoundations of the capabilities necessary to do this. In Teece's words, dynamic capabilities "enable business enterprises to create, deploy, and protect the intangible assets that support superior long-run business performance" (Teece, 2007, p. 1319). Teece proposes a framework that may assist academics in understanding the foundations of long-run enterprise success while helping managers delineate relevant strategic considerations and the priorities they must adopt to enhance enterprise performance and evade ever more competitive global markets warranting competition solely on price.

In their study of the medical technology industry, Bukh and Nielsen (2010) focus on how financial analysts understand the strategy of a healthcare company and which elements, from such a strategy perspective, they perceive as constituting the cornerstone of a healthcare company's business model. The authors analyze whether the characteristics emerging from a comprehensive literature review of the types of information concerning strategy, business models and intellectual capital are reflected in the financial analysts' perceptions of which information is decision relevant and important to communicate to their institutional investor clients. The study illustrates that the analysts and professional investors already have deep insight into a lot of the details of the company, and the most important information is likely to be related to specific strategies and hence difficult to compare across companies and to interpret unless it is disclosed as an integral part of a framework that explains how value is created. Since understanding value configurations and customer value creation is intimately connected with the business model perspective, a possible reconciliation of the reporting–understanding gap could be for the company to communicate about its business model, that is, the story that explains how the enterprise works, who the customer is, and what the customer values – and based on this – determine how the company is supposed to make money. Among Bukh and Nielsen's (2010) conclusions is the importance of distinguishing between the often rather complicated revenue model of the healthcare company and its strategy-oriented business model.

Sustainability might also be interpreted as the propensity to survive and thus also the ability to stay competitive. As such, a business model cannot be a static way of doing business. It must be developed, nursed and optimized continuously in order for the company to meet changing competitive demands. Precisely how the company differentiates itself is the competitive strategy, while it is the business model that defines on which basis this is to be achieved; that is, how it combines its know-how and resources to deliver the value proposition (which will secure profits and thus make the company sustainable).

Once the creative folks have left a business model design process, few people would argue against the necessity of testing and implementing new ideas for business model configurations. By implicitly suggesting that the Strategy Map framework of Kaplan and Norton (2001) is the same as a business model framework (which, according to Nielsen and Roslender (2014), is not an unreasonable assumption), Huelsbeck *et al.* (2011) suggest that firms' business models should be statistically validated to ensure the company is not following a performance measurement system based on erroneous causal assumptions. Huelsbeck *et al.* (2011) are proponents of an analytical approach, and this probably reflects their research perspective. McGrath (2010) takes a somewhat opposing stance to this testing approach in arguing that it is in using the notion of business models to redesign or innovate companies that the contribution lies, because this is a 'discovery driven' rather than an analytical approach to understanding new venture possibilities.

Zott and Amit (2010) stress the importance of locating a focal firm's value creating initiatives within an activity network where the business model describes both intra- and extra-firm relations (i.e. what can be labelled a broad definition of business models). This introduces the notion of an architecture that involves partners in the delivery process of products and services. This framing of business models, in essence, draws up a resource-based approach to the firm but combines this with a transaction costs approach. According to Zott and Amit (2010, p. 218):

A business model is geared toward total value creation for all parties involved. It lays the foundations for the focal firm's value capture by co-defining (along with the firm's products and services) the overall 'size of the value pie', or the total value created in transactions, which can be considered the upper limit of the firm's value capture potential.

It can be argued that a focal firm's business model is driven by value creating initiatives that involve the deployment and articulation of resources, technologies and capabilities to generate products and services. In a seminal piece from 2001, Alt and Zimmermann link the business model to value creation, by stating that the business model is the logic that lies behind the actual processes of a 'business system'.

The speed of change in the business landscape has continuously accelerated. With rising globalization and developments in the BRIC economies ensuring that momentum will continue in the years to come, new forms of value configurations emerge, and with them, probably, so will new types of business models and ways of configuring a company's internal and external architecture. Accordingly, managers as well as industrial and financial analysts must recognize that business models are made up of portfolios of different resources and assets and not merely traditional physical and financial assets, as every company will have created its own specific business model that links its unique combination of assets and activities to value creation.

The rising interest in understanding and evaluating business models can to some extent be traced to the fact that new value configurations outcompete existing ways of doing business. There exist cases where some businesses are more profitable than others in the same industry, even though they apply the same strategy. This would indicate that a business model might well be different from a competitive strategy and a value chain, the latter defined as a set of serially performed activities for a firm in a specific industry, best exemplified by Porter's generic value chain (Porter, 1985) in Figure 17.

According to Sahut *et al.* (2012), business models explain firms' performance as resulting from their heterogeneity, which broadly paves the way for implementing the business model as an explanatory framework for performance. This flow of research intends to clarify how business models facilitate the firm to create and capture value (Amit and Zott, 2001; Chesbrough and Rosenbloom, 2002; Malone *et al.*, 2006; Osterwalder and Pigneur, 2003).

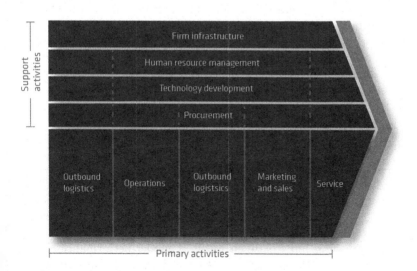

Figure 17 Porter's generic value chain (adapted from Porter, 1985).

Scholars and practitioners have always provided strong implicit assumptions about the nature of performance through divergent interpretations of performance. This is reflected in a tension in business model research between static and dynamic understandings of performance (Demil and Lecocq, 2010). Static performance focuses on value creation and capture (Chesbrough and Rosenbloom, 2002; Teece, 2010). Value creation can be considered the overall value created by a specific firm, while value capture focuses on the economic wealth a firm is able to retain for itself. However, value creation is less debated among scholars. In some contexts, value creation can be assessed by using non-financial metrics such as ratings by critics, or the points obtained by a team in a sports championship (McNamara *et al.*, 2013).

Value capture, in contrast, is much more developed in the literature. Value capture at firm level is based on financial values and ratios. Net income (McNamara *et al.*, 2013; Zott *et al.*, 2011), return on sales (ROS), return on total assets (ROA), compound annual growth rates (CAGRs), inventory turnover (Morris *et al.*, 2013), real profits (Brea-Solís *et al.*, 2015) and market value of equity have been analyzed to measure expected future firm-level value capture (Zott and Amit, 2007, 2008).

According to Demil and Lecocq (2010), the dynamic perspective links business model performance to long-term firm survival, focusing on firms' sustainability, flexibility, adaptability and resilience over time. The existing literature points out that business models can have a strong and positive impact on sustainable competitive advantage and superior financial performance (Amit and Zott, 2001). Several investigations are based on qualitative methodologies, generally involving case studies that sometimes fail to generalize results (Malone *et al.*, 2006; Zott and Amit, 2007).

Transformative redefinition: relevant fourth stage business model research paths

- Research should focus on establishing relationships between business model elements and existing core metrics of financial value and value creation in financial terms, such as suggested by Nielsen and Roslender (2015) who look at return on investment and Economic Value Added[TM] as such potential frameworks.
- Establishing links between business model performance and a broader understanding of performance measure identification will support the connection to managerial issues raised in Chapter 4.

- There is an urgent need to focus better on interrelationships among components of business models, where combinations of resource and activities, instead of features of single components, determine firm performance. The explanation of differences discovered between clusters will facilitate the determination of primary areas in which a firm's key competencies should be developed.
- When analyzing the business model of a firm, there is a need to expand and detail the characteristics of each model component. This would allow the discovery of additional distinctions in firm performance depending on the company business models within a relatively homogeneous cluster of companies.

9 Concluding remarks

The business model field is a field of followers. New themes and topics seem to be driven largely by practitioner insights and 'gurus' from adjacent fields who enter the field with pre-existing perspectives. Our SLR finds that the core academic business model community is not the proactive driver of themes and theorizing; rather, it is the practitioner community. Our analyses depict the contours of a field that has reached maturity and where dominant authors are not critiqued; or if so, then at least the critique has limited impact.

According to Zott *et al.* (2011, p. 1038), there are "at least three concepts that might warrant distinct consideration: (1) e-business model archetypes, (2) business model as activity system, and (3) business model as cost/revenue architecture". Our insights suggest a counter-argument to this view. First, e-business is shown to be an outdated research topic; second, activity systems have already been widely addressed in the second and third research stages of business model research; and third, the value capture perspective of cost/revenue architectures are only a fragmented attempt at understanding the performative notions of business models (Nielsen *et al.*, 2017), which, in following the definition by Osterwalder and Pigneur (2010), must encompass the notions of value creation and value delivery in addition to this value capture perspective. This same line of reasoning is argued by Wirtz *et al.* (2016b).

Our study here provokes a new set of research questions, based on the four identified stages of business model research, which are expected to add to the knowledge base of this vibrant research field. These questions are addressed in the concluding passages of Chapters 5–8, and our hope is that scholars and practitioners of business models will use these as points of departure for seeking out new knowledge and building new perspectives.

Bibliography

Afuah, A., and Tucci, C.L. (2000). *Internet business models and strategies: Text and cases.* McGraw-Hill Higher Education, New York.

Al-Debei, M.M., and Avison, D. (2010). Developing a unified framework of the business model concept. *European Journal of Information Systems,* Vol. 19, No. 3, pp. 359–376.

Alt, R., and Zimmermann, H.-D. (2001). Preface: Introduction to special section. *Business Models, Electronic Markets,* Vol. 11, No. 1, pp. 1–7.

Alt, R., and Zimmermann, H.-D. (2014). Electronic markets and business models. *Electronic Markets,* Vol. 24, No. 4, pp. 231–234.

Alvesson, M., and Deetz, S. (2000). *Doing critical management research.* Sage, London.

Altman, R. (2008). *Theory of narrative.* Columbia University Press, New York.

Amberg, M., and Schröder, M. (2007). E-business models and consumer expectations for digital audio distribution. *Journal of Enterprise Information Management,* Vol. 20, No. 3, pp. 291–303.

Amit, R., and Zott, C. (2001). Value creation in e-business. *Strategic Management Journal,* Vol. 22, Nos 6–7, pp. 493–520.

Amit, R., and Zott, C. (2010). *Business model innovation: Creating value in times of change.* Working Paper, No. WP-870, IESE Business School, Spain.

Amit, R., and Zott, C. (2012). Creating value through business model innovation. *MIT Sloan Management Review,* Vol. 53, No. 3, pp. 41–49.

Ammar, O. (2006). *Strategy and business models: Between confusion and complementarities.* Paper presented to the 22th EGOS Colloquium, Bergen, Norway.

Anderson, B., Johannesson, P., and Zdravkovic, J. (2009). Aligning goals and services through goal and business modeling. *Information Systems E-Business Management,* Vol. 7, No. 2, pp. 143–169.

Andersson, T., Gleadle, P., Haslam, C., and Tsitsianis, N. (2010). Bio-pharma: A financialized business model. *Critical Perspectives on Accounting,* Vol. 21, No. 7, pp. 631–641.

Andersson, T., Lee, E., Theodosopoulos, G., Yin, Y.P., and Haslam, C. (2014). Accounting for the financialized UK and US national business model. *Critical Perspectives on Accounting,* Vol. 25, No. 1, pp. 78–91.

Andrews, K.R. (1971). *The concept of corporate strategy.* Taylor & Francis, New York.

Andrews, K.R. (1980). *The concept of corporate strategy.* Richard D. Irwin, Homewood, AL.

Ansoff, I. (1965). *Corporate strategy.* McGraw-Hill, New York.

Arend, R.J. (2013). The business model: Present and future – beyond a skeumorph. *Strategic Organization*, Vol. 11, No. 3, pp. 390–402.

Arthur, J.B. (1994). Effects of human resource systems on manufacturing performance and turnover. *Academy of Management Journal*, Vol. 37, No. 3, pp. 670–687.

Aspara, J., Hietanen, J., and Tikkanen, H. (2010). Business model innovation vs. replication: Financial performance implications of strategic emphases. *Journal of Strategic Marketing*, Vol. 18, No. 1, pp. 39–56.

Austin, J.E. (2000). Strategic collaboration between nonprofits and businesses. *Nonprofit and Voluntary Sector Quarterly*, Vol. 29, No. 1, pp. 69–97.

Baden-Fuller, C., and Haefliger, S. (2013). Business models and technological innovation. *Long Range Planning*, Vol. 46, No. 6, pp. 419–426.

Baden-Fuller, C., and Mangematin, V. (2013). Business models: A challenging agenda. *Strategic Organization*, Vol. 11, No. 4, pp. 418–427.

Baden-Fuller, C., and Morgan, M.S. (2010). Business models as models. *Long Range Planning*, Vol. 43, Nos 2–3, pp. 156–171.

Bailey, K.D. (1994). *Typologies and taxonomies: An introduction to classification techniques.* Sage Publications, Los Angeles, CA.

Bambury, P. (1998). A taxonomy of Internet commerce. *First Monday*, Vol. 3, No. 10. http://ojphi.org/ojs/index.php/fm/article/view/624 (Accessed September 26, 2018).

Barney, J.B. (1991). Firm resources and sustained competitive advantage. *Journal of Management*, Vol. 17, pp. 99–120.

Batonda, G., and Perry, C. (2003). Approaches to relationship development processes in inter-firm networks. *European Journal of Marketing*, Vol. 37, No. 10, pp. 1457–1484.

Beattie, V., and Pratt, K. (2002). *Voluntary annual report disclosures: What users want.* Institute of Chartered Accountants of Scotland, Edinburgh.

Bell, T., and Solomon, I. (2002). *Cases in strategic-systems auditing.* KPMG LLP, Chicago, IL.

Bell, T., Marrs, F., Solomon, I., and Thomas, H. (1997). *Auditing organizations through a strategic-systems lens: The KPMG business measurement process.* KPMG LLP, Chicago, IL.

Bellman, R., Clark, C.E., Malcolm, D.G., Craft, C.J., and Ricciardi, F.M. (1957). On the construction of a multi-stage, multi-person business game. *Operations Research*, Vol. 5, No. 4, pp. 469–503.

Betz, F. (2002). Strategic business models. *Engineering Management Journal*, Vol. 14, No. 1, pp. 21–27.

Bigliardi, B., Nosella, A., and Verbano, C. (2005). Business models in Italian biotechnology industry: A quantitative analysis. *Technovation*, Vol. 25, No. 11, pp. 1299–1306.

Björkdahl, J. (2009). Technology cross-fertilization and the business model: The case of integrating ICTs in mechanical engineering products. *Research Policy*, Vol. 38, No. 9, pp. 1468–1477.

Blank, S. (2013). *The four steps to the epiphany: Successful strategies for products that win.* K & S Ranch Press, Pescadero, CA.

Blank, S. (2013). Why the lean start-up changes everything. *Harvard Business Review*, Vol. 91, No. 5, pp. 63–72.

Blumenberg, H., and Wallace, R.M. (1985). *Work on myth.* MIT Press, Cambridge, MA.

Bock, A., Opsahl, T., and George, G. (2010). *Business model innovation and strategic flexibility: A study of the effects of informal and formal organisation.* Working Paper No. SSRN 1533742, Imperial College London.

Bock, A.J., Opsahl, T., George, G., and Gann, D.M. (2012). The effects of culture and structure on strategic flexibility during business model innovation. *Journal of Management Studies*, Vol. 49, No. 2, pp. 279–305.

Bocken, N., Short, M.P., Rana, S.W., and Evans, P. (2014). A literature and practice review to develop sustainable business model archetypes. *Journal of Cleaner Production*, Vol. 65, pp. 42–56.

Bonaccorsi, A., Rossi, C., and Giannangeli, S. (2006). Entry strategies under dominant standards. Hybrid business models in the open source software industry. *Management Science*, Vol. 52, No. 7, pp. 1085–1089.

Bontis, N. (2001). Assessing knowledge assets: A review of the models used to measure intellectual capital. *International Journal of Management Reviews*, Vol. 3, No. 1, pp. 41–60.

Boulton, R.E.S., Libert, B.D., and Samek, S.M. (1997). *Cracking the value code: How successful businesses are creating wealth in the New Economy.* Harper Collins Publishers, New York.

Boulton, R.E.S., Libert, B.D., and Samek, S.M. (2000). A new business model for the new economy. *Journal of Business Strategy*, Vol. 21, No. 4, pp. 29–35.

Bouwman, H., De Vos, H., and Haaker, T. (2008). *Mobile service innovation and business models.* Springer, Heidelberg, Germany.

Bray, M. (2002). *New directions in business: Performance reporting, communication and assurance.* The Institute of Chartered Accountants in Australia, Sydney, NSW.

Brea-Solís, H., Casadesus-Masanell, R., and Grifell-Tatjé, E. (2015). Business model evaluation: Quantifying Walmart's sources of advantage. *Strategic Entrepreneurship Journal*, Vol. 9, No. 1, pp. 12–33.

Brinberg, D., and Hirschman, E.C. (1986). Multiple orientations for the conduct of marketing research: An analysis of the academic/practitioner distinction. *Journal of Marketing*, Vol. 50, No. 4, pp. 161–173.

Brink, J., and Holmen, M. (2009). Capabilities and radical changes of the business models of new bioscience firms. *Creativity and Innovation Management*, Vol. 18, No. 2, pp. 109–120.

Brousseau, E., and Penard, T. (2007). The economics of digital business models: A framework for analyzing the economics of platforms. *Review of Network Economics*, Vol. 6, No. 2, pp. 81–114.

Bruneel, J., D'Este, P., and Salter, A. (2010). Investigating the factors that diminish the barriers to university-industry collaboration. *Research Policy*, Vol. 39, pp. 858–868.

Budde Christensen, T., Wells, P., and Cipcigan, L. (2012). Can innovative business models overcome resistance to electric vehicles? Better place and battery electric cars in Denmark. *Energy Policy*, Vol. 48, pp. 498–505.

Bukh, P.N., and Nielsen, C. (2010). Understanding the health care business model: The financial analyst's point of view. *Journal of Health Care Finance*, Vol. 37, No. 2, pp. 8–25.

Cappelli, P. (2009). The future of the US business model and the rise of competitors. *The Academy of Management Perspectives*, Vol. 23, No. 2, pp. 5–10.

Casadesus-Masanell, R., and Ricart, J.E. (2010). From strategy to business models and onto tactics. *Long Range Planning*, Vol. 43, Nos 2–3, pp. 195–215.

Casadesus-Masanell, R., and Ricart, J.E. (2011) How to design a winning business model. *Harvard Business Review*, Vol. 89, Nos 1/2, pp. 100–107.

Casadesus-Masanell, R., and Zhu, F. (2013). Business model innovation and competitive imitation: The case of sponsor-based business models. *Strategic Management Journal*, Vol. 34, No. 4, pp. 464–482.

Casper, S. (2000). Institutional adaptiveness, technology policy, and the diffusion of new business models: The case of German biotechnology. *Organization Studies*, Vol. 21, No. 5, pp. 887–914.

Certo, S.T., Holcomb, T.R., and Holmes, R.M. (2009). IPO research in management and entrepreneurship: Moving the agenda forward. *Journal of Management*, Vol. 35, No. 6, pp. 1340–1378.

Chaharbaghi, K., Fendt, C., and Willis, R. (2003). Meaning, legitimacy and impact of business models in fast-moving environments. *Management Decision*, Vol. 41, No. 4, pp. 372–382.

Chandler, A.D., Jr. (1962). *Strategy and structure: Chapters in the history of the industrial enterprise*. MIT Press, Cambridge, MA.

Chapman, R.L., Soosay, C., and Kandampully, J. (2002). Innovation in logistic services and the new business model: A conceptual framework. *Managing Service Quality: An International Journal*, Vol. 12, No. 6, pp. 358–371.

Chatterjee, S. (2013). Simple rules for designing business models. *California Management Review*, Vol. 55, No. 2, pp. 97–124.

Chen, S. (2003). The real value of "e-business models". *Business Horizons*, Vol. 46, No. 6, pp. 27–33.

Chesbrough, H. (2003). *Open innovation – The new imperative for creating and profiting from technology*. Harvard Business School Press, Brighton, MA.

Chesbrough, H. (2006). *Open business models: How to thrive in the new innovation landscape*. Harvard Business School Press, Brighton, MA.

Chesbrough, H. (2007a). Business model innovation: It's not just about technology anymore. *Strategy and Leadership*, Vol. 35, No. 6, pp. 12–17.

Chesbrough, H. (2007b). Why companies should have open business models. *MIT Sloan Management Review*, Vol. 48, No. 2, pp. 22–28.

Chesbrough, H. (2010). Business model innovation: Opportunities and barriers. *Long Range Planning*, Vol. 43, Nos 2–3, pp. 354–363.

Chesbrough, H., and Rosenbloom, R.S. (2002). The role of the business model in capturing value from innovation: Evidence from Xerox Corporation's spin-off companies. *Industrial and Corporate Change*, Vol. 11, No. 3, pp. 529–555.

Child, J. (1972). Organizational structure, environment and performance: The role of strategic choice. *Sociology*, Vol. 6, pp. 1–22.

Christensen, C.M. (2001). The past and future of competitive advantage. *Sloan Management Review*, Vol. 42, No. 2, pp. 105–109.

Clark, T., Osterwalder, A., and Pigneur, Y. (2012). *Business model you: A one-page method for reinventing your career.* John Wiley & Sons, New Jersey.

Collinson, E., and Quinn, L. (2002). The impact of collaboration between industry and academia on SME growth. *Journal of Marketing Management*, Vol. 18, Nos 3–4, pp. 415–434.

Cooper, R. (1992). Formal organization as representation: Remote control, displacement and abbreviation, in Reed, M., and Hughes, M. (eds.), *Rethinking organization*, Sage Publications, London, pp. 254–272.

Cooper, R.G. (2008). Perspective: The Stage-Gate® idea-to-launch process – Update, what's new, and NexGen systems*. *Journal of Product Innovation Management*, Vol. 25, No. 3, pp. 213–232.

Costa, C.J., and Aparicio, M. (2004). *Business models for hotspot – An exploratory study.* IADIS International Conference, pp. 915–918 (retrieved from researchgate.net 31.07.2018).

D'Souza, A., Wortmann, H., Huitema, G., and Velthuijsen, H. (2015). A business model design framework for viability: A business ecosystem approach. *Journal of Business Models*, Vol. 3, No. 2, pp. 1–29.

DaSilva, C.M., and Trkman, P. (2014). Business model: What it is and what it is not. *Long Range Planning*, Vol. 47, No. 6, pp. 379–389.

De Carolis, D.M. (2003). Competencies and imitability in the pharmaceutical industry: An analysis of their relationship with firm performance. *Journal of Management*, Vol. 29, No. 1, pp. 27–50.

de Reuver, M., Bouwman, H., and MacInnes, I. (2009). Business model dynamics: A case survey. *Journal of Theoretical and Applied Electronic Commerce Research*, Vol. 4, No. 1, pp. 1–11.

Demil, B., and Lecocq, X. (2010). Business model evolution: In search of dynamic consistency. *Long Range Planning*, Vol. 43, Nos 2–3, pp. 227–246.

Denning, S. (2005). Mastering the discipline of business narrative. In *An Advance Copy of an Article in Strategy and Leadership* (retrieved from stevedenning.com 31.07.2018).

DeYoung, R. (2005). The performance of Internet-based business models: Evidence from the banking industry. *The Journal of Business*, Vol. 78, No. 3, pp. 893–948.

Doganova, L., and Eyquem-Renault, M. (2009). What do business models do? Innovation devices in technology entrepreneurship. *Research Policy*, Vol. 38, No. 10, pp. 1559–1570.

Donaldson, T., and Preston, L.E. (1995). The stakeholder theory of the corporation: Concepts, evidence, and implications. *Academy of Management Review*, Vol. 20, No. 1, pp. 65–91.

Doty, D.H., and Glick, W.H. (1994). Typologies as a unique form of theory building: Toward improved understanding and modelling. *Academy of Management Review*, Vol. 19, No. 2, pp. 230–251.

Doz, Y.L., and Kosonen, M. (2010). Embedding strategic agility – A leadership agenda for accelerating business model renewal. *Long Range Planning*, Vol. 43, Nos 2–3, pp. 370–382.

Drucker, P.F. (1993). *Concept of the Corporation*. Transaction Publishers.

Dubosson-Torbay, M., Osterwalder, A., and Pigneur, Y. (2002). E-business model design, classification, and measurements. *Thunderbird International Business Review*, Vol. 44, No. 1, pp. 5–23.

Dumay, J. (2014). 15 years of the journal of intellectual capital and counting: A manifesto for transformational IC research. *Journal of Intellectual Capital*, Vol. 15, No. 1, pp. 2–37.

Dunford, R., Palmer, I., and Benveniste, J. (2010). Business model replication for early and rapid internationalisation: The ING Direct experience. *Long Range Planning*, Vol. 43, Nos 5–6, pp. 655–674.

Dyer, J., and Singh, H. (1998). The relational view: Cooperative strategy and sources of interorganizational competitive advantage. *The Academy of Management Review*, Vol. 23, No. 4, pp. 660–679.

Eccles, R., and Mavrinac, S. (1995). Improving the corporate disclosure process. *Sloan Management Review*, Vol. 36, No. 4, pp. 11–25.

Eriksson, C., Kalling, T., Åkesson, M., and Fredberg, T. (2008). Business models for M-services: Exploring the E-newspaper case from a consumer view. *Journal of Electronic Commerce in Organizations*, Vol. 6, No. 2, pp. 29–57.

Eustace, C. (2000). *The intangible economy-impact and policy issues*. European Commission, Brussels.

Evans, P.B., and Wurster, T.S. (1997). Strategy and the new economics of information. *Harvard Business Review*, Vol. 75, No. 5, pp. 70–82.

Eyring, M.J., Johnson, M.W., and Nair, H. (2011). New business models in emerging markets. *Harvard Business Review*, Jan–Feb, pp. 89–95.

Faucher-King, F. (2008). The "modernization" of the labour party, 1994–2007: The successes and difficulties of importing the business model in politics. *Politix*, Vol. 21, No. 81, p. 125.

Feng, H., Froud, J., Johal, S., Haslam, C., and Williams, K. (2001). A new business model? The capital market and the new economy. *Economy and Society*, Vol. 30, No. 4, pp. 467–503.

Fenigstein, T. (2003). *Issues arising in the valuation of hi-tech companies*. PricewaterhouseCoopers LLP, London.

Ferry, A. (2010). What business model for development in rare diseases? Economic interest versus social responsibility? *Presse Medicale*, Vol. 39, No. 5, pp. 56–58.

Fielt, E. (2014). Conceptualising business models: definitions, frameworks and classifications. *Journal of Business Models*, Vol. 1, No. 1, pp. 85–105.

Fiet, J.O., and Pankaj, C.P. (2008). Forgiving business models for new ventures. *Entrepreneurship Theory and Practice*, Vol. 32, No. 4, pp. 749–761.

Flouris, T., and Walker, T. (2007). Financial comparisons across different business models in the Canadian airline industry. *Journal of Air Transportation*, Vol. 12, No. 1, pp. 25–52.

Foss, N.J., and Saebi, T. (2017). Fifteen years of research on business model innovation: How far have we come, and where should we go? *Journal of Management*, Vol. 43, No. 1, pp. 200–227.

Frankenberger, K., Weiblen, T., and Gassmann, O. (2013). Network configuration, customer centricity, and performance of open business models: A solution provider perspective. *Industrial Marketing Management*, Vol. 42, No. 5, pp. 671–682.

Freeman, R. (1984). *Strategic management: A stakeholder approach*. Pitman, Boston, MA.

Gallaugher, J.M. (2002). E-commerce and the undulating distribution channel. *Communications of the Association for Computing Machinery*, Vol. 45, No. 7, pp. 89–95.

Galper, J. (2001). Three business models for the stock exchange industry. *Journal of Investing*, Vol. 10, No. 1, pp. 70–78.

Gambardella, A., and McGahan, A.M. (2010). Business-model innovation: General purpose technologies and their implications for industry structure. *Long Range Planning*, Vol. 43, Nos 2–3, pp. 262–271.

Garcia, R., and Calantone, R. (2002). A critical look at technological innovation typology and innovativeness terminology: A literature review. *Journal of Product Innovation Management*, Vol. 19, No. 2, pp. 110–132.

Garten, J.E. (2001). Strengthening financial markets: Do investors have the information they need? *Report of an SEC-Inspired Task Force*, Yale School of Management, New Haven, CT.

Gassmann, O., Frankenberger, K., and Csik, M. (2014). *The business model navigator*. Pearson, Harlow.

Gebauer, J., and Ginsburg, M. (2003). The US wine industry and the internet: An analysis of success factors for online business models. *Electronic Markets*, Vol. 13, No. 1, pp. 59–66.

Gelb, D.S. (2002). Intangible assets and firms' disclosures: An empirical investigation. *Journal of Business Finance and Accounting*, Vol. 29, Nos 3–4, pp. 457–476.

George, G., and Bock, A.J. (2011). The business model in practice and its implications for entrepreneurship research. *Entrepreneurship Theory and Practice*, Vol. 35, No. 1, pp. 83–111.

Ghaziani, A., and Ventresca, M.J. (2005). Keywords and cultural change: Frame analysis of business model public talk, 1975–2000. *Sociological Forum*, Vol. 20, No. 4, pp. 523–559.

Giesen, E., Riddleberger, E., Christner, R., and Bell, R. (2010). When and how to innovate your business model. *Strategy and Leadership*, Vol. 38, No. 4, pp. 17–26.

Gnatzy, T., and Moser, R. (2012). Scenario development for an evolving health insurance industry in rural India: INPUT for business model innovation. *Technological Forecasting and Social Change*, Vol. 79, No. 4, pp. 688–699.

Grant, R.M. (1996). Towards a knowledge-based theory of the firm. *Strategic Management Journal*, Vol. 17, No. 2, pp. 109–122.

Grbich, C. (1999). *Qualitative research in health. An introduction.* Allen and Unwin, St Leonards, NSW.

Griss, M.L., Jacobson, I., and Jonsson, P. (1998). Software reuse: Architecture, process and organization for business success. *TOOLS*, Vol. 26, p. 465.

Groth, P., and Nielsen, C. (2015). Constructing a business model taxonomy: Using statistical tools to generate a valid and reliable business model taxonomy. *Journal of Business Models*, Vol. 3, No. 1, pp. 4–21.

Ha, L., and Ganahl, R. (2004). Webcasting business models of clicks-and-bricks and pure-play media: A comparative study of leading webcasters in South Korea and the United States. *International Journal on Media Management*, Vol. 6, Nos. 1–2, pp. 74–87.

Hall, J., and Wagner, M. (2012). Integrating sustainability into firm's processes: Performance effects and the moderating role of business models and innovation. *Business Strategy and the Environment*, Vol. 21, No. 3, pp. 183–196.

Hamel, G. (2000). *Leading the revolution.* Harvard Business School Press, Boston, MA.

Hand, J.R.M. (2001). *Evidence on the winner-takes-all business model: The profitability returns-to-scale of expenditures on intangibles made by U.S. internet firms, 1995–2001.* Working paper, Kenan-Flagler Business School.

Hart, C. (1998). *Doing a literature review: Releasing the social science research imagination.* Sage Publications, London.

Hart, S., and Milstein, M. (2003). Creating sustainable value. *Academy of Management Executive*, Vol. 17, No. 2, pp. 56–67.

Haslam, C., Gleadle, P., Andersson, T., and Tsitsianis, N. (2010). Bio-pharma: A financialized business model. *Critical Perspectives on Accounting*, Vol. 21, No. 7, pp. 631–641.

Haslam, C., Tsitsianis, N., Andersson, T., and Yin, Y.P. (2013). *Redefining business models: Strategies for a financialized world.* Routledge, London.

Hawkins, R. (2002). The phantom of the marketplace: Searching for new e-commerce business models. *Communications & Strategies*, Vol. 46, No. 2, pp. 297–329.

Hedman, J., and Kalling, T. (2001). *The business model: A means to understand the business context of information and communication technology.* School of Economics and Management, Lund University.

Hedman, J., and Kalling, T. (2003). The business model concept: Theoretical underpinnings and empirical illustrations. *European Journal of Information Systems*, Vol. 12, No. 1, pp. 49–59.

Heikkilä, M., Solaimani, S., Soudunsaari, A., Hakanen, M., Kuivaniemi, L., and Suoranta, M. (2014). Performance estimation of networked business models: Case study on a Finnish ehealth service project. *Journal of Business Models*, Vol. 2, No. 1, pp. 71–88.

Helfat, C.E., Finkelstein, S., Mitchell, S., Peteraf, M.A., Singh, H., Teece, D.J., and Winter, S.G. (2007). *Dynamic capabilities: Understanding strategic change in organisations*. Blackwell, New York.

Hienerth, C., Keinz, P., and Lettl, C. (2011). Exploring the nature and implementation process of user-centric business models. *Long Range Planning*, Vol. 44, No. 5–6, pp. 344–374.

Hitt, M.A., Ireland, R.D., Camp, S.M., and Sexton, D.L. (2001). Guest editors' introduction to the special issue strategic entrepreneurship: Entrepreneurial strategies for wealth creation. *Strategic Management Journal*, Vol. 22, Nos 6–7, pp. 479–491.

Hodgkinson, G.P., Herriot, P., and Anderson, N. (2001). Re-aligning the stakeholders in management research: Lessons from industrial, work and organizational psychology. *British Journal of Management*, Vol. 12, S1, pp. S41–S48.

Hoerl, R. (1999). Using an effective business model for group practice management. *Healthcare Financial Management*, Vol. 53, No. 11, pp. 61–62.

Holland, J.B. (1997). *Corporate communications to institutional shareholders*. ICAS Research Report, Edinburgh.

Huelsbeck, D.P., Merchant, K.A., and Sandino, T. (2011). On testing business models. *The Accounting Review*, Vol. 86, No. 5, pp. 1631–1654.

Huff, A.S. (2000). Citigroup's John Reed and Stanford's James March on management research and practice. *Academy of Management Executive*, Vol. 14, No. 1, pp. 52–64.

Iivari, M.M. (2015). Dynamics of openness in SMEs: A business model and innovation strategy perspective. *Journal of Business Models*, Vol. 3, No. 2, pp. 30–50.

Iivari, M.M., Ahokangas, P., Komi, M., Tihinen, M., and Valtanen, K. (2016). Toward ecosystemic business models in the context of industrial internet. *Journal of Business Models*, Vol. 4, No. 2, pp. 42–59

Itami, H., and Nishino, K. (2010). Killing two birds with one stone – Profit for now and learning for the future. *Long Range Planning*, Vol. 43, Nos 2–3, pp. 364–369.

Jacobides, M.G., Knudsen, T., and Augier, M. (2006). Benefiting from innovation: Value creation, value appropriation and the role of industry architectures. *Research Policy*, Vol. 35, No. 8, pp. 1200–1221.

Janasz, T. (2017). *Paradigm shift in urban mobility: Towards factor 10 of automobility*. Springer, London.

Jensen, A.B. (2014). Do we need one business model definition. *Journal of Business Model*, Vol. 1, No. 1, pp. 61–84.

Johansson, M., and Abrahamsson, J.T. (2014). Competing with the use of business model innovation – An exploratory case study of the journey of born global firms. *Journal of Business Models*, Vol. 2, No. 1 pp. 33–55.

Johnson, M., Christensen, C.M., and Kagermann, H. (2008). Reinventing your business model. *Harvard Business Review*, Vol. 86, No. 12, pp. 50–59.

Johnson, M.W. (2010). *Seizing the white space.* Harvard Business Press, Boston, MA.

Jones, G.M. (1960). Educators, electrons, and business models: A problem in synthesis. *The Accounting Review*, Vol. 35, No. 4, pp. 619–626.

Kaplan, R.S., and Norton, D.P. (2001). *The strategy-focused organization.* Harvard Business School Press, Boston, MA.

Kaplan, S. (2011). Business models aren't just for business. *Harvard Business Review.* http://blogs.hbr.org/2011/04/business-models-arent-just-for/ (Accessed September 09, 2017).

Katkalo, V.S. (2008). *The evolution of strategic management theory.* Graduate School of Management Publications, St. Petersburg State University Press.

Keen, P., and Qureshi, S. (2006). *Organizational transformation through business models: A framework for business model design.* Paper presented at the 39th Annual Hawaii International Conference on System Sciences, Kauai, HI, 4–7 January.

Ketokivi, M., and Choi, T. (2014). Renaissance of case research as a scientific method. *Journal of Operations Management*, Vol. 32, No. 5, pp. 232–240.

Kind, H.J., Nilssen, T., and Sorgard, L. (2009). Business models for media firms: Does competition matter for how they raise revenue? *Marketing Science*, Vol. 28, No. 6, pp. 1112–1128.

Kodama, M. (1999). Customer value creation through community-based information networks. *International Journal of Information Management*, Vol. 19, No. 6, pp. 495–508.

Kozberg, A. (2001). *The value drivers of internet stocks: A business models approach.* Working paper, Zicklin School of Business, CUNY – Baruch College.

KPMG (2001). *Achieving measurable performance improvement in a changing world: The search for new insights.* Assurance and Advisory Services Center, KPMG LLP, London.

Kraemer, K.L., Dedrick, J., and Yamashiro, S. (1999). *Refining and extending the business model with information technology: Dell Computer Corporation.* White paper, Center for Research on Information Technology and Organizations.

Krippendorff, K. (2013). *Content analysis. An introduction to its methodology.* Sage Publications, Thousand Oaks, CA.

Kristiansen, K.B., Nielsen, C., Tange, K., Laursen, F., and Oehlenschläger, J. (2015). Kickass companies: Leveraging business models with great leadership. *Journal of Business Models*, Vol. 3, No. 1, pp. 22–28.

Lambert, S. (2006). *Do we need a general classification scheme for e-business models?* ACIS 2006 Proceedings. 36. http://aisel.aisnet.org/acis2006/36.

Lambert, S., and Montemari, M. (2017). Business model research: From concepts to theories. *International Journal of Business and Management*, Vol. 12, No. 11, p. 41.

Lambert, S.C. (2015). The importance of classification to business model re-search. *Journal of Business Models*, Vol. 3, No. 1, pp. 49–61.

Lambert, S.C., and Davidson, R.A. (2013). Applications of the business model in studies of enterprise success, innovation and classification: An analysis of empirical research from 1996 to 2010. *European Management Journal*, Vol. 31, No. 6, pp. 668–681.

Latour, B. (1999). *Pandora's hope – Essays on the reality of science studies.* Harvard University Press, Boston, MA.

Lawton, T.C., and Solomko, S. (2005). When being the lowest cost is not enough: Building a successful low-fare airline business model in Asia. *Journal of Air Transport Management*, Vol. 11, No. 6, pp. 355–362.

Leblebici, H. (2012). The evolution of alternative business models and the legitimization of universal credit card industry: Exploring the contested terrain where history and strategy meet, in Kahl, S.J., Silverman, B.S., and Cusumano, M.A. (eds.), *History and strategy* (*Advances in strategic management*, Vol. 29), Emerald Group Publishing Limited, Bradford, pp. 117–151.

Lee, S. (2001). *Financial analysts' perception on intangibles: An interview survey in Finland.* ETLA Discussion Paper No. 778.

Lee, Y., Shin, J., and Park, Y. (2012). The changing pattern of SME's innova-tiveness through business model globalisation. *Technological Forecasting and Social Change*, Vol. 79, No. 5, pp. 832–842.

Leitch, T.M. (1986). *What stories are: Narrative theory and interpretation.* Pennsylvania State University Press, University Park.

Lev, B. (2001). *Intangibles – Management, measuring and reporting.* Brookings Institution Press, Washington, D.C.

Lewin, K. (1946). Action research and minority problems. *Journal of Social Issues*, Vol. 2, pp. 34–46.

Linder, J., and Cantrell, S. (2000). Changing business models: Surveying the land-scape. *Accenture*. 34 (retrieved from http://scholar.google.com/scholar?hl=enandbtnG=Searchandq=intitle:Changing+Business+Models:+Surveying+the+Landscape#0, 1 March 2015).

Linder, J., and Cantrell, S. (2002). What makes a good business model any-way? Can yours stand the test of change? *Outlook*, www.accenture.com.

Lund, M., and Nielsen, C. (2014). The evolution of network-based business models illustrated through the case study of an entrepreneurship project. *Journal of Business Models*, Vol. 2, No. 1, pp. 105–121.

Lunn, M. (2002). Using business models and revenue streams for digital mar-ketplace success. *Information Management and Computer Security*, Vol. 10, No. 1, pp. 20–27.

Lüttgens, D., and Diener, K. (2016). Business model patterns used as a tool for creating (new) innovative business models. *Journal of Business Models*, Vol. 4, No. 3, pp. 48–67.

Magretta, J. (2002). Why business models matter. *Harvard Business Review*, Vol. 80, No. 5, pp. 86–92.

Mahadevan, B. (2000). Business models for internet-based e-commerce: An anatomy. *California Management Review*, Vol. 42, No. 4, pp. 55–69.

Mäkinen, S., and Seppänen, M. (2007). Assessing business model concepts with taxonomical research criteria: A preliminary study. *Management Research News*, Vol. 30, No. 10, pp. 735–748.

Malone, T., Weill, P., Lai, R., D'Urso, V., Herman, G., Apel, T., and Woerner, S. (2006). *Do some business models perform better than others?* MIT Sloan Research Paper No. 4615–06. Available at SSRN: https://ssrn.com/abstract=920667.

Manafy, M. (2006). Time for a business-model remix? Music distribution in the wake of the Sony BMG DRM debacle. *EContent-Digital Content Strategies and Resources*, Vol. 29, No. 1, pp. 8–10.

Mansfield, G.M., and Fourie, L.C.H. (2004). Strategy and business models – Strange bedfellows? A case for convergence and its evolution into strategic architecture. *South African Journal of Business Management*, Vol. 35, No. 1, pp. 35–44.

Marrs, F.O., and Mundt, B.M. (2001). Enterprise concept: Business modeling analysis and design, in Salvendy, G. (ed.), *Handbook of industrial engineering: Technology and operations management*. John Wiley & Sons, New York, pp. 26–60.

Mason, K.J., and Leek, S. (2008). Learning to build a supply network: An exploration of dynamic business models. *Journal of Management Studies*, Vol. 45, No. 4, pp. 774–799.

Massa, L., Tucci, C.L., and Afuah, A. (2017). A critical assessment of business model research. *Academy of Management Annals*, Vol. 11, No. 1, pp. 73–104.

Massaro, M., Dumay, J., and Garlatti, A. (2015). Public sector knowledge management: A structured literature review. *Journal of Knowledge Management*, Vol. 19, No. 3, pp. 530–558.

Massaro, M., Dumay, J.C., and Guthrie, J. (2016a). On the shoulders of giants: Undertaking a structured literature review in accounting. *Accounting, Auditing and Accountability Journal*, Vol. 29, No. 5, pp. 767–901.

Massaro, M., Handley, K., Bagnoli, C., and Dumay, J. (2016b). Knowledge management in small and medium enterprises. A structured literature review. *Journal of Knowledge Management*, Vol. 20, No. 2, pp. 258–291.

Mayes, C. (2010). *The archetypal hero's journey in teaching and learning: A study in Jungian pedagogy*. Atwood Publishing, Madison.

Mayo, M.C., and Brown, G.S. (1999). Strategic Planning: The business model: Relied upon for years, the traditional business model is on shaky ground. *Ivey Business Journal*, Vol. 63, pp. 18–23.

McClean, S.T. (2007). *Digital storytelling: The narrative power of visual effects in film*. MIT Press, Boston, MA.

McGrath, R.G. (2010). Business models: A discovery driven approach. *Long Range Planning*, Vol. 43, pp. 247–261.

McKelvey, B. (1982). *Organizational systematics: Taxonomy, evolution, classification*, University of California Press, Berkeley, CA.

McNamara, P., Peck, S.I., and Sasson, A. (2013). Competing business models, value creation and appropriation in English football. *Long Range Planning*, Vol. 46, No. 6, pp. 475–487.

Michea, A. (2016). *Enacting business models: An ethnographic study of an emerging business model innovation within the frame of a manufacturing company.* Ph.D. thesis, Copenhagen Business School.

Miles, S. (2012). Stakeholder: Essentially contested or just confused? *Journal of Business Ethics*, Vol. 108, No. 3, pp. 285–298.

Minkler, M., and Wallerstein, N. (eds.) (2003). *Community-based participatory research for health.* Jossey-Bass, San Francisco, CA.

Montemari, M., and Chiucchi, M.S. (2017). Enabling intellectual capital measurement through business model mapping: The Nexus case, in Guthrie, J., Dumay, J., Ricceri, F., and Nielsen, C. (eds.), *The routledge companion to intellectual capital*, Routledge, London, pp. 266–283.

Morris, L. (2003). *Business model warfare: The strategy of business breakthroughs.* InnovationLabs and A-CASA, University of Pennsylvania, Philadelphia.

Morris, M., Schindehutte, M., and Allen, J. (2005). The entrepreneurs business model: Toward a unified perspective. *Journal of Business Research*, Vol. 58, pp. 726–735.

Morris, M.H., Shirokova, G., and Shatalov, A. (2013). The business model and firm performance: The case of Russian food service ventures. *Journal of Small Business Management*, Vol. 51, No. 1, pp. 46–65.

Moyon, E., and Lecocq, X. (2010). Co-evolution between stages of institutionalization and agency: The case of the music industry's business model. *Management International/Gestiòn Internacional/International Management*, Vol. 14, No. 4, pp. 37–53.

Mullins, J.W., and Komisar, R. (2009). *Getting to plan B: Breaking through to a better business model.* Harvard Business Press, Boston, MA.

Neuman, W.L. (2003). *Social research methods: Qualitative and quantitative approaches (5th Edition).* Pearson Education Inc., Boston, MA.

Nielsen, C. (2005). *Modelling transparency: A research note on accepting a new paradigm in business reporting (No. M-2005-03).* University of Aarhus, Aarhus School of Business, Department of Business Studies.

Nielsen, C. (2010). *Conceptualizing, analyzing and communicating the business model.* Aalborg University, Department of Business Studies, Working Paper Series, No. 2.

Nielsen, C., and Montemari, M. (2012). The role of human resources in business model performance: the case of network-based companies. *Journal of Human Resource Costing & Accounting*, Vol. 16, No. 2, pp. 142–164.

Nielsen, C., and Bukh, P.N. (2011). What constitutes a business model: The perception of financial analysts. *International Journal of Learning and Intellectual Capital*, Vol. 8, No. 3, pp. 256–271.

Nielsen, C., and Roslender, R., Frameworks for understanding and describing business models, in Nielsen, C., and Lund, M. (eds.), *The basics of business models*, BookBoon.com/Ventus Publishing Aps, Copenhagen. pp. 55–74.

Nielsen, C., and Lund, M. (2018). Building scalable business models. *MIT Sloan Management Review*, Vol. 59, No. 2, pp. 65–69.

Nielsen, C., Lund, M., and Thomsen, P. (2017). Killing the balanced scorecard to improve internal disclosure. *Journal of Intellectual Capital*, Vol. 18, No. 1, pp. 45–62.

Nielsen, C., and Roslender, R. (2015). Enhancing financial reporting: The contribution of business models. *British Accounting Review*, Vol. 47, No. 3, pp. 262–274.

Nielsen, C., Roslender, R., and Bukh, P.N. (2009). Intellectual capital reporting: Can a strategy perspective solve accounting problems? in Lytras, M., and Ordóñez de Pablos, P. (eds.), *Knowledge ecology in global business: Managing intellectual capital*, Information Science Reference, Hershey, pp. 174–191.

Normann, R. (2001). *Reframing business: When the map changes the landscape*. John Wiley & Sons, New York.

Nunes, P., and Breene, T. (2011). Reinvent your business before it's too late: Watch out for those S curves. *Harvard Business Review*, Jan–Feb, pp. 80–87.

Olejnik, E. (2014). *International small and medium-sized enterprises*. Springer Gabler, Trier, Germany.

Onetti, A., Zucchella, A., Jones, M.V., and McDougall-Covin, P.P. (2012). Internationalization, innovation and entrepreneurship: Business models for new technology-based firms. *Journal of Management Governance*, Vol. 16, pp. 337–368.

O'Reilly, T. (2007). What is web 2.0: Design patterns and business models for the next generations software. *International Journal of Digital Economics*, No. 65, pp. 17–37.

Osterwalder, A. (2001). *An e-Business model ontology for the creation of new management software tools and IS requirement engineering*. Working paper, Ecole des HEC, University of Lausanne.

Osterwalder, A. (2004). *The business model ontology – A proposition in a design science approach*. Ph.D. thesis, Universite de Lausanne, Ecole des Hautes Etudes Commerciales, Switzerland.

Osterwalder, A., and Pigneur, Y. (2003). *Towards business and information systems fit through a business model ontology*. Working paper, Ecole des HEC, University of Lausanne.

Osterwalder, A., and Pigneur, Y. (2010). *Business model generation: A handbook for visionaries, game changers, and challengers*. John Wiley & Sons, Hoboken, New Jersey.

Osterwalder, A., Pigneur, Y., Bernarda, G., and Smith, A. (2014). *Value proposition design: How to create products and services customers want*. John Wiley & Sons, Hoboken, New Jersey.

Osterwalder, A., Pigneur, Y., and Tucci, C. (2005). Clarifying business models: Origins, present, and future of the concept. *Communications of the Association for Information Systems*, Vol. 15, No. 1, pp. 1–43.

Ozanne, J.L., and Saatcioglu, B. (2008). Participatory action research. *Journal of Consumer Research*, Vol. 35, No. 3, pp. 423–439.

Palenzuela, D.R. (2001). Sources of economic renewal: From the traditional firm to the knowledge firm. *European Central Bank Working Paper Series*, Working Paper no. 43.

Pateli, A.G., and Giaglis, G.M. (2004). A research framework for analysing eBusiness models. *European Journal of Information Systems*, Vol. 13, pp. 302–314.

Penrose, E.T. (1959). *The theory of the growth of the firm.* John Wiley & Sons, New York.

Perkmann, M., and Spicer, A. (2010). *What are business models? Developing a theory of performative representations.* AIM Research Working Paper Series.

Petrovic, O., Kittl, C., and Teksten, R.D. (2001). *Developing business models for eBusiness* (retrieved from https://ssrn.com/abstract=1658505).

Pisano, G.P. (1994). Knowledge, integration, and the locus of learning: An empirical analysis of process development. *Strategic Management Journal*, Vol. 15, No. 2, pp. 85–100.

Pitelis, C.N. (2009). The co-evolution of organizational value capture, value creation and sustainable advantage. *Organization Studies*, Vol. 30, No. 10, pp. 1115–1139.

Porter, M.E. (1985). *Competitive advantage: Creating and Sustaining Superior Performance.* Free Press, New York.

Porter, M.E. (1991). Towards a dynamic theory of strategy. *Strategic Management Journal*, Vol. 12, pp. 95–117.

Porter, M.E. (1996). What is strategy? *Harvard Business Review*, Vol. 74, No. 6, pp. 61–78.

Porter, M.E. (2001). Strategy and the Internet. *Harvard Business Review*, Vol. 79, No. 3, pp. 62–78.

Prahalad, C.K., and Bettis, R.A. (1986). The dominant logic: A new linkage between diversity and performance. *Strategic Management Journal*, Vol. 7, No. 6, pp. 485–501.

Prahalad, C.K., and Hammond, A. (2002). Serving the world's poor, profitably. *Harvard Business Review*, Vol. 80, No. 9, pp. 4–11.

Prahalad, C.K., and Hart, S.L. (2002). The fortune at the bottom of the pyramid. *Strategy and Business*, Vol. 26, No. 1, pp. 2–14.

Ramirez, R. (1999). Value co-production: Intellectual origins and implications for practice and research. *Strategic Management Journal*, Vol. 20, pp. 49–65.

Rappa, M. (2001). *Managing the digital enterprise – Business models on the Web*, North Carolina State University, Raleigh (retrieved from http://ecommerce.ncsu.edu/business_models.html).

Rappa, M.A. (2004). The utility business model and the future of computing services. *IBM Systems Journal*, Vol. 43, No. 1, pp. 32–42.

Reason, P., and Bradbury, H (2001). *Handbook of action research: Participative inquiry and practice.* Sage Publications, London.

Richardson, J. (2008). The business model: An integrative framework for strategy execution. *Strategic Change*, Vol. 17, Nos 5–6, pp. 133–144.

Ries, E. (2011). *The lean startup: How today's entrepreneurs use continuous innovation to create radically successful businesses.* Crown Publishing, New York.

Sabatier, V., Craig-Kennard, A., and Mangematin, V. (2012). When technological discontinuities and disruptive business models challenge dominant industry logics: Insights from the drugs industry. *Technological Forecasting and Social Change*, Vol. 79, No. 5, pp. 949–962.

Sahut, J.M., Hikkerova, L., and Khalfallah, M. (2012). Business model and performance of firms. *International Business Research*, Vol. 6, No. 2, p. 64.

Samuels, A., Shorter, B., and Plaut, F. (1986). *A critical dictionary of Jungian thought.* Routledge & Kegan Paul, New York.

Sanchez, P., and Ricart, J.E. (2010). Business model innovation and sources of value creation in low-income markets. *European Management Review*, Vol. 7, No. 3, pp. 138–154.

Sandberg, K.D. (2002). Is it time to trade in your business model? *Harvard Management Update*, Vol. 7, No. 1, pp. 3–6.

Sax, B. (2006). Storytelling and the "information overload". *On the Horizon*, Vol. 14, No. 4, pp. 165–170.

Schaltegger, S., Hansen, E.G., and Lüdeke-Freund, F. (2016). Business models for sustainability: Origins, present research, and future avenues. *Organization & Environment*, Vol. 29, No. 1, pp. 3–10.

Schmid, B.F. (2001). What is new about the digital economy? *Electronic Markets*, Vol. 11, No. 1, pp. 44–51.

Schneider, S., and Spieth, P. (2013). Business model innovation: Towards an integrated future research agenda. *International Journal of Innovation Management*, Vol. 17, No. 1, pp. 1–34.

Schüle, S., Schubert, M., Hoyer, C., and Dressel, K.M. (2016). Development of an assessment tool to evaluate and improve SME business models. *Journal of Business Models*, Vol. 4, No. 3, pp. 5–18.

Schumpeter, J.A. (1942). *Capitalism, socialism, and democracy.* Harper, New York.

Seddon, P.B., Lewis, G.P., Freeman, P., and Shanks, G. (2004). The case for viewing business models as abstractions of strategy. *Communications of the Association for Information Systems*, Vol. 13, pp. 427–442.

Seelos, C., and Mair, J. (2005). Social entrepreneurship: Creating new business models to serve the poor. *Business Horizons*, Vol. 48, No. 3, pp. 241–246.

Seelos, C., and Mair, J. (2007). Profitable business models and market creation in the context of deep poverty: A strategic view. *The Academy of Management Perspectives*, Vol. 21, No. 4, pp. 49–63.

Selz, D. (1999). *Value webs: Emerging forms of fluid and flexible organizations*, Ph.D. thesis, der Universitat St. Gallen.

Senge, P.M., and Carstedt, G. (2001). Innovating our way to the next industrial revolution. *MIT Sloan Management Review*, Vol. 42, No. 2, pp. 24–38.

Serenko, A., Bontis, N., Booker, L., Sadeddin, K., and Hardie, T. (2010). A scientometric analysis of knowledge management and intellectual capital academic literature 1994–2008. *Journal of Knowledge Management*, Vol. 14, No. 1, pp. 3–23.

Shafer, S.M., Smith, H.J., and Linder, J.C. (2005). The power of business models. *Business Horizons*, Vol. 48, No. 3, pp. 199–207.

Shi, Y., and Manning, T. (2009). *Understanding business model and business model risk.* École Universitaire de Management, Working Paper.

Shipley, T. (1995). *IS needs multiple business models.* Research Note Gartner Group, Doc. No. SPA-MGT-1177 (retrieved from www.gartnergroup.com 25 September 2000).

Simon, H.A. (1962). The architecture of complexity. *Proceedings of the American Philosophical Society*, Vol. 106, pp. 467–482.

Simon, H.A. (1973). The structure of ill-structured problems. *Artificial Intelligence*, Vol. 4, pp. 181–201.

Sirmon, D.G., Hitt, M.A., and Ireland, R.D. (2007). Managing firm resources in dynamic environments to create value: Looking inside the black box. *Academy of Management Review*, Vol. 32, No. 1, pp. 273–292.

Skarzynski, P., and Gibson, R. (2008). *Innovation to the core.* Harvard Business School Publishing, Boston, MA.

Slywotsky, A.J. (1996). *Value migration.* Harvard Business Review Press, Boston, MA.

Smith, W.K., Binns, A., and Tushman, M.L. (2010). Complex business models: Managing strategic paradoxes simultaneously. *Long Range Planning*, Vol. 43, Nos 2–3, pp. 448–461.

Sosna, M., Trevinyo-Rodríguez, R.N., and Velamuri, S.R. (2010). Business model innovation through trial-and-error learning: The Naturhouse case. *Long Range Planning*, Vol. 43, Nos 2–3, pp. 383–407.

Sovinc, A. (2009). Secovlje Salina Nature Park, Slovenia – New business model for preservation of wetlands at risk. Global NEST. *The International Journal*, Vol. 11, No. 1, pp. 19–23.

Spieth, P., Schneckenberg, D., and Ricart, J.E. (2014). Business model innovation – State of the art and future challenges for the field. *R&D Management*, Vol. 44, No. 3, pp. 237–247.

Stabell, C.B., and Fjeldstad, Ø.D. (1998). Configuring value for competitive advantage: On chains, shops and networks. *Strategic Management Journal*, Vol. 19, pp. 413–437.

Stähler, P. (2002). *Business models as a unit of analysis for strategizing.* Paper presented at the 1st International Workshop on Business Models, Lausanne, 4–5 October.

Stanzel, F.K. (1986). *A theory of narrative.* Cambridge University Press, Cambridge.

Starbuck, W.H., and Dutton, J.M. (1973). Designing adaptive organizations. *Journal of Business Policy*, Vol. 3, pp. 21–28.

Stewart, D.W., and Zhao, Q. (2000). Internet marketing, business models, and public policy. *Journal of Public Policy and Marketing*, Vol. 19, No. 2, pp. 287–296.

Sugiyama, M.S. (2001). Narrative theory and function: Why evolution matters. *Philosophy and Literature*, Vol. 25, No. 2, pp. 233–250.

Sveiby, K.E. (2012). Innovation and the global financial crisis – Systemic consequences of incompetence. *International Journal of Entrepreneurship and Innovation Management*, Vol. 16, Nos 1–2, pp. 30–50.

Svejenova, S., Slavich, B., and Abdel-Gawad, S. (2012). Business models of creative entrepreneurs: The case of haute cuisine chefs, in Jones, C., Lorenzen, M. and Sapsed, J. (eds.), *Handbook of creative industries*, Oxford University Press, Oxford, pp. 184–199.

Swatman, P.M.C., Krueger, C., and Van Der Beek, K. (2006). The changing digital content landscape: An evaluation of e-business model development in European online news and music. *Internet Research*, Vol. 16, No. 1, pp. 53–80.

Sweet, P. (2001). Strategic value configuration logics and the 'new' economy: A service economy Revolution? *International Journal of Service Industry Management*, Vol. 12, No. 1, pp. 70–83.

Tapscott, D., Lowy, A., and Ticoll, D. (2000). *Digital capital: Harnessing the power of business webs.* Harvard Business School Press, Brighton, MA.

Taran, Y., Nielsen, C., Montemari, M., Thomsen, P., and Paolone, F. (2016). Business model configurations: A five-V framework to map out potential innovation routes. *European Journal of Innovation Management*, Vol. 19, No. 4, pp. 492–527.

Teece, D.J. (1984). Economic analysis and strategic management. *California Management Review*, Vol. 36, No. 3, pp. 172–194.

Teece, D.J. (2007). Explicating dynamic capabilities: The nature and microfoundations of (sustainable) enterprise performance. *Strategic Management Journal*, Vol. 28, No. 13, pp. 1319–1350.

Teece, D.J. (2010). Business models, business strategy and innovation. *Long Range Planning*, Vol. 43, Nos 2–3, pp. 172–194.

Thierry, V., and Jouison-Laffitte, E. (2009). *The business model, a relevant concept in the entrepreneurship training.* University Pole of Management Science (PUSG), Bordeaux, France.

Thompson, J.D. (1967). *Organizations in action: Social science bases of administrative theory.* McGraw-Hill, New York.

Tikkanen, H., Lamberg, J.A., Parvinen, P., and Kallunki, J.P. (2005). Managerial cognition, action and the business model of the firm. *Management Decision*, Vol. 43, No. 6, pp. 789–809.

Timmers, P. (1998). Business models for electronic markets. *Electronic Markets*, Vol. 8, No. 2, pp. 3–8.

Tretheway, M.W. (2004). Distortions of airline revenues: Why the network airline business model is broken. *Journal of Air Transport Management*, Vol. 10, No. 1, pp. 3–14.

Tweedie, D., Nielsen, C., and Martinov-Bennie, N. (2017). The business model in Integrated Reporting: Evaluating concept and application. *Australian Accounting Review* (e-Pub ahead of print).

Vardi, N. (2010). Al Qaeda's new business model. *Forbes*, Vol. 185, No. 3, pp. 60–66.

Velocci, A.L. (2001). New business model taking root around closer collaboration. *Aviation Week & Space Technology*, Vol. 155, No. 16, pp. 72–74.

Venkatraman, N., and Henderson, J.C. (1998). Real strategies for virtual organizing. *Sloan Management Review*, Vol. 40, No. 1, pp. 33–48.

Verhoeven, B., and Johnson, L.W. (2017). Business model innovation portfolio strategy for growth under product-market configurations. *Journal of Business Models*, Vol. 5, No. 1, pp. 35–50.

Verstraete, T., and Jouison-Laffitte, E. (2011). *A business model for entrepreneurship*. Edward Elgar Publishing, London.

Von Bertalanffy, L. (1951). Problems of general system theory. *Human Biology*, Vol. 23, No. 4, p. 302.

Von Krogh, G., and Roos, J. (1995). A perspective on knowledge, competence and strategy. *Personnel Review*, Vol. 24, No. 3, pp. 56–76.

Weill, P., and Vitale, M.R. (2001). *Place to space: Migrating to eBusiness models*. Harvard Business School Press, Boston, MA.

Wernerfelt, B. (1984). A resource-based view of the firm. *Strategic Management Journal*, Vol. 5, No. 2, pp. 171–180.

Williamson, O.E. (1975). *Markets and hierarchies, analysis and antitrust implications: A study in the economics of internal organization*. Free Press, New York.

Wirtz, B.W., Göttel, V., and Daiser, P. (2016a). Business model innovation: Development, concept and future research directions. *Journal of Business Models*, Vol. 4, No. 2, pp. 1–28.

Wirtz, B.W., Pistoia, A., Ullrich, S., and Göttel, V. (2016b). Business models: Origin, development and future research perspectives. *Long Range Planning*, Vol. 49, No. 1, pp. 36–54.

Wirtz, B.W., Schilke, O., and Ullrich, S. (2010). Strategic development of business models: Implications of the Web 2.0 for creating value on the internet. *Long Range Planning*, Vol. 43, Nos 2–3, pp. 272–290.

Yip, G. (2004). Using strategy to change your business model. *Business Strategy Review*, Vol. 15, No. 2, pp. 17–24.

Yunus, M., Moingeon, B., and Lehmann-Ortega, L. (2010). Building social business models: Lesson from the Grameen experience. *Long Range Planning*, Vol. 43, Nos 2–3, pp. 308–325.

Zalewska-Kurek, K., Kandemir, S., Englis, B.G., and Englis, P.D. (2016). Development of market-driven business models in the IT industry. How firms experiment with their business models? *Journal of Business Models*, Vol. 4, No. 3, pp. 48–67.

Zott, C., and Amit, R. (2007). Business model design and the performance of entrepreneurial firms. *Organization Science*, Vol. 18, No. 2, pp. 181–199.

Zott, C., and Amit, R. (2008). The fit between product market strategy and business model: Implications for firm performance. *Strategic Management Journal*, Vol. 29, No. 1, pp. 1–26.

Zott, C., and Amit, R. (2010). Business model design: An activity system perspective. *Long Range Planning*, Vol. 43, Nos 2–3, pp. 216–226.

Zott, C., and Amit, R. (2013). The business model: A theoretically anchored robust construct for strategic analysis. *Strategic Organization*, Vol. 11, No. 4, pp. 403–411.

Zott, C., Amit, R., and Massa, L. (2011). The business model: Recent developments and future research. *Journal of Management*, Vol. 37, No. 4, pp. 1019–1042.

Zuboff, S. (1988). *In the age of the smart machine: The future of work and power.* Basic Books, New York.

Index

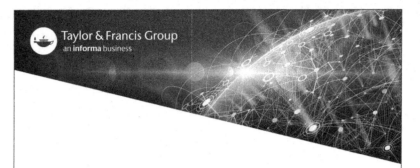

Printed in the United States
by Baker & Taylor Publisher Services